Martin H. Manser has been a professional reference book editor since 1980. He has compiled or edited more than 150 reference books, particularly English language dictionaries, thesauruses and Bible reference titles. He is also a language trainer and consultant with national companies and organizations.

www.martinmanser.com

Prayers for Good Times and Grim

Martin H. Manser

MONARCH
B O O K S

Oxford, UK & Grand Rapids, Michigan, USA

First published in the UK in 2008 by Monarch Books
(a publishing imprint of Lion Hudson plc),
Wilkinson House, Jordan Hill Road, Oxford OX2 8DR.
Tel: +44 (0)1865 302750 Fax: +44 (0)1865 302757
Email: monarch@lionhudson.com
www.lionhudson.com

ISBN: 978-1-85424-861-9 (UK)
ISBN: 978-0-8254-6193-4 (USA)

Distributed by:
UK: Marston Book Services Ltd, PO Box 269, Abingdon, Oxon OX14 4YN;
USA: Kregel Publications, PO Box 2607, Grand Rapids, Michigan 49501

Unless otherwise stated, Scripture quotations are taken from the Holy
Bible, New International Version, © 1973, 1978, 1984 by the International
Bible Society. Used by permission of Hodder & Stoughton Ltd. All rights
reserved.

This book has been printed on paper and board independently certified as
having come from sustainable forests.

Illustrations by Fred Apps.

British Library Cataloguing Data
A catalogue record for this book is available from the British Library.

Printed and bound in China.

Contents

Acknowledgments

Many people have helped in compiling this book. I would like to express my appreciation to Tony Collins who encouraged me to undertake it. My twin sister Ros, and friends (Peter Arthern, Jeff Ballantine, Rosalind Desmond, Ester Rothery, Bernard Harlock, Michael and Jeanette Hulcoop, Beccy Sargeant, Angela and Robin Scott, Peter Smith, Liz Stoddard, Janet Sunman) checked through some of the prayers and I'm very grateful for their comments. Ros and her husband Steve and my cousins Cathy and Colin provided quietness to pray and write. My secretary Inna deciphered my handwriting and my wife Yusandra provided warm and loving encouragement. I'm grateful to you all: thank you!

Martin H. Manser

6

Introduction

A few years ago James, the six-year-old son of a friend at church, came up to me and said, 'I don't believe in Jesus any more.' I was taken aback by his comment but on reflection I was grateful for James' disarming honesty – he put into words what I sometimes feel. Some days, when everything is going fine, it's easy to believe in God. We're thrilled with the privilege of knowing God and can express ourselves easily to him. On other days, when things are going badly, it's more difficult. Then, prayer may seem as hard work as wading through treacle. I've compiled this book of honest prayers – thoughts to God expressed from the heart – to help us in times when we find it difficult to pray. Those times could be days of grave crisis but also times when we feel spiritually dry, when we don't quite know what to say, and we need some help to get us started.

The best way to learn how to pray is to pray. There is no one right way, no set formula. Prayer is expressing ourselves to God; it's about saying 'Help!', it's about saying 'Thank you', 'Please', 'Sorry', and expressing our love for him. It's also about asking 'Why?' in difficult times. (To pursue this thought, see also Martin Manser and Mike Beaumont, *The Eagle Handbook of Bible Prayers*, Bath: Eagle, 2002).

If you want to know how to begin, thank God for what

you have, what you can see around you – the sky, the snow, the blossom, the sun, the autumn colours. Talk to him naturally and honestly about the concerns you have: the big things such as people's illnesses, and the small things such as finding somewhere to park the car. Be yourself; be natural.

You can pray anywhere – at your desk, in an armchair, in the supermarket, on the bus, in a plane. You can pray at any time – first thing in the morning, at lunchtime, on your way home, at night. You can pray about anything – from the crises facing the world through the needs of your community to your own personal life.

Many people find it helpful to read the Bible alongside praying. God speaks to us through his word, and then we respond to him in prayer. If you are new to the Bible, a good place to start is one of the Gospels: Mark is easy to get into. The Psalms express a wide range of emotions and can be a useful help in personal prayer. (See also Martin Manser, *Treasury of Psalms*, Oxford: Lion, 2003).

Above all, I believe prayer is a relationship each one of us can have with God through Jesus Christ. I hope this collection will help you in your own adventure with him.

Martin H. Manser
May 2008

1

Prayers in Difficult Times

When you feel afraid

Lord, I'm scared stiff.

Even the thought of what I'm going to have to go through makes my heart stop.

Help me to rest in all of who you are, in your person, in Christ and all his power.

My emotional tank is on 'empty'; I desperately need you.

Help!

When you feel angry

I'm absolutely livid, Lord!

How could they have said that to me... done that to me?

Don't they know I have feelings too? I feel really fed up with the way they've treated me.

And to think we used to be close friends!

I'm not sure whether I want to mend this relationship, Lord – although I know the theory about loving others...

And yet, Lord, I sense you breaking in right now: You really want me to love my enemies? Wow! How? Lord, that seems completely impossible right now.

Lord, if possible, please soften my anger, soften my heart. May there be a reconciliation, a meeting of common minds.

Help, Lord!

When you feel confused

Lord, I feel confused. Whichever way I turn, I don't know what to do.

I know the theory, Lord; you say you are in control, but I'm having real problems working it out in practice right now.

I am trying to remember you are with me. Wherever I am; on a train, on a plane, in my office or at the kitchen sink, you are with me.

Help me to really trust that you are in control of my life. Help me to know your support, to be still and depend on you more and more fully... to *know* – above all the other voices that swirl around in me, and which threaten to overwhelm me, in the fog I feel I'm in – to *know* that you truly and really are God... the Lord of *my* life.

I thought you wanted me to go in that direction in my life. I pushed open the door but everything went pear-shaped and I feel I'm in an even worse state now than I was before.

I feel everyone is looking at me and thinking bad thoughts of me: 'They said they trusted God but look where it's got them!'

Lord, I feel such a fool. Please help me out of this mess.

I thank you I can pour out my heart to you.

May I learn to remember who you are, to focus on you and not on myself, to see again your greatness, to remember you are faithful.

Lord, as I look back on the past I thank you that you have always provided for me, even in unexpected ways. Lord, I want to praise you, even though I don't feel like doing so.

Deepen my trust in you, even though I don't feel you are near. I remember that you came to help the weak, guide the bewildered, and encourage those who realize their need of you.

Come to me, Lord, I pray.

Please give me clarity about what to do, how to balance everything in my life, all the demands that are being made on me, as I juggle all the different responsibilities I feel I have to fulfil.

Please give me courage to make decisions and do what I believe – what you show me – to be right. Lord, I pray the decisions will be the right ones, but even if they're not quite right, please overrule and lead me deeper into the plans you have for my life.

Lord, I give myself to you afresh. Quieten me and be Lord of my life again right now, I pray. Amen.

When feeling critical

Lord, I'm sorry I feel so judgmental, so critical of others, so inclined to find fault with what everyone else is and does.

Help me to turn away from myself and to see people as you do... human beings made in your image.

Lord, I repent of my critical attitude. Please give me grace to have a right sense of others. May I realize again that it is only you who can truly judge people.

Lord, far from judging others and acting critically towards them, may I support them in love. Please show me practical ways in which I can express your kindness towards them.

In Christ's name I pray. Amen.

When you feel depressed

I feel isolated, Lord. You seem a million miles away. At times I can't stop myself crying; I feel so overwhelmed, worn out and torn apart. Everything has got on top of me. To be honest, I don't know who to turn to. I don't feel really close to anyone; there's no one I can open up to and say what's really going on inside me.

Lord, I know the theory! You're supposed to be my rock, but all the bottled-up feelings are still there.

There were, of course, the good old days when my faith – and perhaps it was that rather than you – kept me going, smiling happily and not letting anything bother me.

Lord, if you could help me to be a little less preoccupied with myself I'd be so thankful. May I learn to think, to realize that feelings aren't facts, to be realistic, to know I can't change the world overnight. Lord, help me to be patient with those around me... my circumstances... and also myself. Help me to be firm, too, Lord, if possible, to move on and move out from the endless despair I feel I'm stuck in right now.

May I remember again, you sympathize with and understand what I am going through – that, Lord Jesus, you felt abandoned on the cross...

Please restore in me the right perspective on life. Help me to control my anxieties. Give me people I can really talk to.

Please come and help me, Lord. Give me strength for one day at a time.

When you feel disappointed

Lord, I feel you have let me down.

I thought you promised me great things but they've not worked out. I prayed, but nothing seemed to happen.

It's a terrible thing to say or even think but I feel you've betrayed me. I thought I'd fulfilled my part but you've not 'come up with the goods'; I don't think you've delivered your side of the bargain. You've not answered my prayers.

Your words sucked me in and made me submit... but what did I get for it? But Lord, I sense you are teaching me new things – even deeper, wider things. You want me to move beyond my hurt and anger, to turn away from my self-pity, and turn back to you.

Lord, restore me, save me, give me a fresh vision of yourself that is immeasurably wider than the little circle I've drawn around myself.

Give me grace to accept what has happened and to learn from it. Thank you that your grace is sufficient for all my needs.

Lord, I do want to serve you again, to live for you, to be strong for you.

Please come and save me in Christ's name. Amen.

When doubting

Lord, I'm not sure any more.

Are you really there?

Some days I'm as certain of you as I'm sitting here now. But at other times my faith wavers. It seems to be as light and thin as a piece of tissue paper.

There seem to be so many questions; the world is full of uncertainties. Why are babies born deformed? Why do innocent people suffer? Why is there so much injustice in the world? Why do police officers get killed? Why are there earthquakes? Why do planes crash? The list could go on and on, Lord...

Help me look beyond my lack of faith to you, to see the 'bigger picture' of you.

Thank you that I do have faith that is small, even though it seems to be as small as a grain of sand. Even though that is so tiny, may that be built on today.

'Lord, I believe a little; help me to believe more.'

Before a driving test

Help me, Lord, today when I take my test. Give me concentration. I pray about the traffic lights – I want them all to be green (although I know they won't be), but I pray they won't change suddenly as I drive up to them.

And I pray for all the traffic on the roundabouts.

I pray for my examiner. May they be fair towards me. Lord, you know I want to pass this exam, so I ask for your help. In Jesus' name. Amen.

Before an exam

Lord, you know my thoughts are centred on the exam I've got in a few hours.

Even as I think about it – and you know I've not thought about anything else all night – there's an uneasy feeling in the pit of my stomach.

You know I've done some revision – but not nearly enough! – and I just feel so badly prepared.

Lord, *please* may some of the questions I've revised come up in the exam.

Help me, Lord, to remember all the facts I've learned; help me to concentrate and do justice to the abilities you've given me and the work and the revision I have done.

Lord, I need to know your overruling, sovereign hand on my life.

Help, Lord!

When you have failed

Lord, I've messed up big time. How come I never seem to learn from my past mistakes? I feel awful.

I said the wrong things; I put my foot in it by speaking without having first stopped to think. I wish I could take back my words. Help me to control my words in future.

I did the wrong things.

My thoughts were a million miles from you.

I freely admit I'm a complete failure.

Help me to stop and realize your love again.

Thank you that you do not condemn me.

May I know afresh that Christ died on the cross for me to take away my selfishness, the blame I deserve, and the penalty of all the wrongs of the world, including mine.

In Jesus' name I pray. Amen.

When God seems far away

Why, Lord, am I going through this time of dryness and emptiness? This desert experience?

How long will it last, Lord?

When will I know again the warm assurance and sense of your presence?

Lord Jesus, I remember you were led by the Spirit into the desert. May I become quiet enough to hear your still small voice, your gentle tones.

I sense, Lord, that in this desert experience you are lightening my load, showing me what is really important in life. Maybe, too, Lord, you are preparing me for some fresh challenge. Teach me the lessons you want me to learn here about yourself, about my relationship with you and with others. May I come to focus again on the true values of life. Refine me, Lord, I pray.

May I come close to you and experience your friendship.

May I learn to depend only on you and give myself to you afresh, I pray.

When you need forgiveness

Lord God, I recognize that my wrongdoing, my wrong thinking, my wrong being – my sin – has come between me and you. I confess and admit my sin. I ask you to cleanse and forgive me.

I thank you, heavenly Father, that you are rich in mercy, that you are full of compassion. I kneel before the cross again and see how terrible my sin is... how I have defied you and rebelled against you. I thank you that Christ died to take away the punishment that was due to fall on me. I remember again that Jesus Christ died on the cross to bring me forgiveness, to restore my relationship with you. I thank you that you rescue me, you deliver me. I receive Christ's forgiveness again now, as a free gift. I thank you that I can know peace with God through our Lord Jesus Christ.

May I walk afresh now in the joy of your salvation, humbly grateful for your salvation, sensitive again to the calls of discipleship and enjoying all that you give me as one of your children. Amen.

When needing guidance

Lord, you know that I need guidance at this time. I thank you that I know you are the good shepherd, and that you will certainly show me the way through the confusion I seem to be in.

Lord Jesus, sometimes I feel as if I'm alone on a cold, dark night. I don't know which way to turn. Help me to trust in you even when the glimmer of light seems so dim, faint and far away and I hardly know what to do.

Lord, teach me your way. Show me what to do, as I consider all the circumstances surrounding the decision I need to make. May I follow the clear directions from your word, the Bible. May I discern afresh the way of your Spirit as I listen to those who know me well.

As I pray, may I listen out for you and know you are with me. And Lord, even if I don't fully sense your peace and assurance before I make the decision, please show me the way. Overrule if the decision I make isn't quite right, and bring glory to Christ in every part of my life, I pray.

Help me to come to know you more deeply so that I may discern more clearly the way you want me to follow. Amen.

When you feel guilty

Lord, I know I shouldn't have...

I see it as wrong now, but I didn't at the time... it kind of just happened and now I have to face up to the consequences...

I'm sorry that I thought I could get away with it.

Lord, I realize I've sinned against people, but even more deeply, I've sinned against you. 'I am guilty.' There, I've said it. I've broken your law; I've offended your holy justice.

I am guilty in your law court.

I need your cleansing. Cleanse me, wash me thoroughly inside; may I come to know you more fully again. I need to be made whole once more. I need your radical surgery – a clean heart – deep inside me, not just a sticking plaster on a surface scratch.

I cry out to you for your forgiveness. I thank you that Christ paid the ultimate price for the sins of the world – for the sins of bad people everywhere, for *my* sins... for *that* sin. May I accept your forgiveness for that sin right now.

Help me, too, to put things right with the people I've offended, to sort out this mess... to think and act clearly and in the truly right way. Give me the courage and power to do what I need to.

Lord, help me at this time, I pray. Amen.

When you feel ill

Lord, I feel so helpless. This illness came on me so suddenly. I can't believe it. I realize how I've taken health for granted – I'm sorry for that, Lord: forgive me, I pray.

Now, Lord, I thank you for the doctors and nurses who are looking after me.

Help me to be patient as I look to you for healing and recovery. Please work naturally through the care, medicine, and surgery, and also supernaturally by the Spirit of Christ himself to bring wholeness.

Lord, may I be comfortable and be at peace with you.

I pray, too, for others who are ill. May they get better, too, Lord. I pray, in Christ's name. Amen.

When you feel impatient

Lord, I'm so impatient. Nothing seems to be going my way: everything seems to be against me, from traffic lights through computers and supermarket queues to relationships. There seems to be no end to it.

Thank you that you are patient ... with me and everyone in the world. Thank you that you do not deal with us according to what we deserve. May I learn to trust you more, in all that you are, in your timing, in your justice, in your love that never fails.

Lord, help me to become just a little less restless!

I pray in Christ's name. Amen.

When you feel insecure

Lord, I think you are the only one who knows the inner insecurities I try to hide from others. You see through the mask I wear in front of them. I thank you that I can open up to a few close friends about my innermost feelings, about my fears, hurtful events and difficult people in my past, where I am too sensitive or feel threatened.

May I know that I am safe in your hands. Help me to trust in you, my strong tower.

I remember again that all my hope is set on you. Protect me from fears, from the attacks of Satan. Keep me trusting in Jesus Christ, and may I know more of the fullness of your love in me, driving out my fears and insecurities.

Help me to know your love poured out again into my life, into my innermost being, to fill up all the cracks of my insecurities and make me whole in you. In Jesus' name I pray. Amen.

When you feel jealous

Lord, you know I'm incredibly jealous of the people around me... their friends, their nice house, their secure job, their well-behaved children.

Help me to become free from these thoughts, Father, for I recognize they are self-centred and sinful.

Save me from comparing myself with others all the time. Teach me a new lesson in humility and in accepting what I have – what you have given me – and the circumstances I find myself in. Amen.

When you feel lonely

Lord, I feel so desperately lonely. I feel I've got no close friends around me. They've all moved away and I seem to know no one deeply at all... no one I can be myself with.

Please help me to remember you are with me always – yes, even now, that nothing can separate me from your love. May I sense your close presence afresh. But, Lord, I pray also that you will bring people across my path who can be supportive. May I be a friend to others, Lord, and in so doing may I make new friends. In Christ's name I pray. Amen.

When needing peace

Lord, I feel my life is like a rough sea – troubled, angry, upset. My emotions are like the waves: all up and down, agitated and choppy.

I desperately need your peace. Come alongside me to help me. May I sense again your own comfort, strength and encouragement. Quieten my feelings. Calm the waters of my spirit. Pour your soothing Spirit into my inner being once again, I humbly ask, in Jesus' name. Amen.

When feeling proud

Forgive me, Lord, for my pride. I'm aware that I've got 'too big for my boots'. I've become overconfident of my own achievements and I've left you out of the picture.

Lord, I know you hate people who are proud, who do not depend on you, who think they can get by without you. I know you will humble me, you will 'bring me down a peg or two'. Make me teachable and sensitive to you and others.

May I learn to have a modest, honest, right assessment of myself. May I learn again to glory only in your power, the power of God: the power of the cross, the power of the gospel, the power of the Spirit.

God, I beg you to be merciful to me, a sinner.

When you need help in recovering from past hurts

Lord and heavenly Father, you know what has happened in my life... many years ago.

You know how deeply this has affected me over the years.

I thank you that I can talk about this with you.

Lord, please help me recover from this event. Please restore me inwardly, in the deep recesses of my thoughts and emotions. Please bring your healing and your wholeness. Lord, I don't want to be defined by what happened... I want to move on from it.

Lord, please help me to deal with the thoughts of the person who brought this pain on me. I don't want to hold onto anger and bitterness throughout the rest of my life. I want to forgive them, not to continue to hold it against them.

May I accept others' help in my recovery and restoration, too, Lord, I pray.

Lord, I know all good and all power are in you and with you. I need that power and help at this time in my life! Please come, I pray. Heal me throughout my life, Lord Jesus. Amen.

When feeling sad

Lord, I feel so terribly sad. The burden of the illness of those I love is so great, Lord, I feel I'm walking through the valley of the shadow of death.

Lord, life is so difficult at this time. The news always seems so bad... floods, terrorism, murders, plane crashes.

And then Lord, I confess I'm finding the path of discipleship a hard one. Lord, you promised peace, rest and a light burden, but it is weighing down heavily on me right now.

Lord, I turn to you in my sadness. You are the hope of those who grieve. You comfort those who are sad and sorrowful. Even you, Lord Jesus, wept when your friend died. And you knew what it meant to be troubled, overwhelmed and in anguish.

May I know your comfort and strength in my sadness. I thank you that I am not alone: I am grateful for friends around me to encourage me and give me fresh hope for the journey I face with you today and every day. Thank you, Lord Jesus. Amen.

When you feel stressed

Lord, I feel I have taken on far too much. I feel that everything is beginning to fall on top of me. I know I am not coping. I feel I'm losing my grip on reality. I fear that everything I get involved with threatens to overwhelm me, like waves bursting in on a small boat.

Lord, thank you that you understand the situation I'm in. Come into the boat. Calm my body, my mind, my emotions – my nerves! – calm the waters. Speak your words of stillness. May I become more and more aware of the reality of your living presence. May I be sensible, too, Lord, if I need to try to relax more. Help me to make time to unwind and chill out.

Give me fresh courage to face all the tasks before me.

In Christ's name, Amen.

When suffering

Lord, I thank you that you understand what I am going through at this time... the pain, the troubles... the anguish.

Help me to remember that this difficulty will not last for ever – although it is so deep right now and it feels it will continue that way.

I ask you for your help now, heavenly Father. May I know your support, your presence, and even glimpses of your joy breaking in on my experience. May I know again your care for me, your peace, your protection.

Lord, this suffering has brought life into sharp focus. It has made me realize the stark and raw realities of life and death.

Give me light to see that my depression will lift. Give me hope to move beyond my anxiety. Give me faith to trust you really are in control of my life.

Help me to grasp this opportunity to know you more... to know again your courage to serve and love others, even within my limitations.

In Jesus' name I pray. Amen.

When tempted

Lord, you know the temptation I face. May I know your help at this time as I fight it. Its power, its pull, Lord, seems so great. The desire, the attraction seems so magnetic, appealing and alluring.

I thank you, Lord Jesus, that you know what it was like to be tempted… yet you did not sin. I pray for your grace and strength right now to protect me. May I stand strong in you, Lord, the Rock, in your power. May I resist Satan and all his schemes.

Help me to stay alert, watchful, and self-controlled, to have a healthy distrust of my own sinful heart. May I guard my inner life, not cherish *wrong* thoughts. Restrain my words and actions.

May I be sensible, keeping as far away from sin as I can. May I remember I am one of your children, with your Spirit living in me, and to keep my body and all my life holy and pure before you.

May I know the support and help of friends around me to guide me through the difficult times, Lord, I pray.

Please help me, Lord, I humbly ask. Amen.

When feeling tired or weak

Lord, I just feel so worn out. The demands of life are just too much, Lord Jesus. There are so many – far too many! – calls on my time, my energy, my money, my life.

There are the children with all their needs, my parents and all they have to face at this stage in their lives... my work with its ever-increasing duties, and church with all the struggles and responsibilities. Lord, every day is a battle just to get through. I'm not just 'running on empty', Lord, I've completely run out of all the energy within me.

Lord, I don't want to stay in this condition. I turn to you and ask you for your strength, your power. Lord, I just need a fresh fullness of the resources of heaven to come to me right now! Help me to sleep soundly and deeply and to awake refreshed, with the vision and the energy to face a new day.

Lord, I do want to affirm again my trust in you. May I know that I can truly do everything with your strength actively working inside me. It would be wonderful to be able to say that the joy of the Lord is my strength – to be able to say that and really mean it.

When feeling unimportant

Lord, I just feel so unimportant, so insignificant.

Everyone else seems to get the attention, to be in the limelight. I'm left here, Lord, like the last person to be picked for a school team – after all the skilled and popular ones have been chosen.

Lord, sometimes I feel I might as well not be here; no one seems to notice me.

But thank you, Lord, that I know *you* notice me. You have a special place in your heart for the marginalized – those left out.

Please help me not to be so absorbed with myself, so preoccupied with little old me.

Make me look outward to others who I sense also feel left out. May I take you to them as I know you come to me.

I pray in Christ's name. Amen.

When you feel worried and anxious

Lord, I'm so worried... so anxious.

Help me to turn to you right now. Sometimes I'm full of faith in you, and then the next moment I'm overwhelmed with worry... about the future... my children... my parents... the city I live in... the world.

My thoughts are in a spin... my mind is racing away. My stomach is in knots. It's affecting my sleep. I want to escape from my panicky feelings, but I know I can't.

But I thank you, Lord – I can talk to you, even when I can't talk to anyone else. I can still trust you even though the surface of my faith ebbs and flows so much.

Help me to focus again on who you are. May I remember that whatever happens you are *always* with me; may you come to me with your peace and strength. Amen.

2

Prayers in Times of Change

Engagement

Lord, I'm – we're – so excited! It all seemed to happen like a whirlwind. The proposal – the yes! – and now we're engaged!

Thank you so much, Lord, for each other, for *us*, for the way you've made us, for the way you brought us together, for our future lives together – as one.

Lord, as we dream dreams for the future, may we learn together and grow in our respect and love for each other.

In all our excitement about our love, may we draw closer to each other and even closer to you, too. May we not forget you, heavenly Father, the Giver of life and love.

We commit to you our future, Lord. Guide us as we plan the wedding, and as we share our thoughts and hopes – and our fears – with each other.

Thank you for our excitement, Lord God. In Christ's name we pray. Amen.

Wedding

Father in heaven, the great day has come at last! We thank you for the joy, excitement and celebration of this day. We pray that all the arrangements will go OK, that the weather will be fine, that the cars will turn up on time, that the photographer will work out OK.

Thank you so much, Lord, for each other, for us, for the way you've made us, for the way you brought us together, for our future together as one.

Lord Jesus, we remember that you were present at the wedding at Cana in Galilee. May we sense your presence here today, too.

At the heart of the day are our promises to each other. We thank you that you have brought us together. May we know you are with us as we speak out our love, respect and promises to each other. May we know your help in working out the commitments we make to each other today in your presence, and in the presence of our family and friends.

May we remember this day as a special one for the rest of our lives. Lord, as we dream dreams for the future, help us to learn together, to grow in our respect and love for each other, and as we do so, to draw even closer to you.

May our trust in and our love for one another deepen in the years ahead.

Keep us faithful to each other.

May we thank you in the good times. Keep us in the everyday times. Help us in the difficult times of ill health or shaky finances.

Keep us talking to each other and forgiving each other as we grow together in our relationship.

May today be the beginning of the fulfilment of our hopes and dreams. We thank you for all that you have prepared for us, and we look forward to sharing it together, in Jesus' name. Amen.

A new home

A new home... how exciting, Lord!

New adventures, new experiences... rooms to decorate, a space to call my own to get things just as I want them, a garden to tend, somewhere I can create my own identity.

Thank you for all the possibilities, Lord. I pray for happy times here, with family and friends.

And, Lord, please help me get rid of some of the junk I've accumulated over the years. Make my life simpler!

At this time of move, may I also have a 'spring-clean' of my own life to draw closer to you. May I get rid of some of the clutter that slows down my spiritual life.

Lord Jesus, I give you this new home. Come into it by your Spirit. May he fill every room. And I come to you with my life, too, Lord. I give my life again to you. Come and fill me afresh with your living Spirit in every area of my life.

In Jesus' name. Amen.

Birth

Heavenly Father, Creator of life, we thank you for the birth of our newborn child.

We thank you for their well-formed body, for their good health. We recognize you as the One who has given life, breath and everything.

We thank you for all the staff in the hospital and the community, the midwife, the doctors and nurses who have helped us so far on our journey. We thank you for the joy and happiness we feel at this time.

And now, Lord, as we have our newborn child, we

thank you for them. We pray that this child will grow up well, that we will give them deep love and security in these early months of their life, that they will be safe, whole and happy.

May they learn to love life. May they come to know you personally and accept you as Saviour and Lord.

May they discover all the gifts you have for them. May they fulfil the potential you have for them; may they become the whole people you intend them to be.

Lord, give us wisdom as we care for our newborn baby. We acknowledge our dependence on you to be patient and persevere, to know which way to turn, to be helped in all the choices and decisions we will need to make in the future.

Guide us as a family; give us strength for each day. We ask in Jesus' name. Amen.

Starting school

Lord, as our son/daughter begins school today, we pray for them, we thank you for them, for the gift of life you have given them.

We thank you for their growth, their good health, their individual personality – the way you have made them.

We pray that as they set out on the road of learning today, may they discover the adventure of life for themselves. May they be safe. May they have fun. May they learn new skills as well as new facts. May they learn to listen, to care and to work hard. May they be happy and more and more secure in your love, as they grow up into mature adults.

May they build firm foundations for their lives that will keep them strong in all the ups and downs of life in the future.

We pray, too, for all their teachers and helpers, that you will help them to look after the children in their school.

In Jesus' name. Amen.

Starting at a new school

Lord, I'm so nervous and scared. You know I'm moving to a new school. I feel as if I'm the only one who won't know anyone. I might go to the wrong room, say the wrong thing or do the wrong thing – the teachers might not be very nice to me.

Help me to settle in and to make new friends quickly, I pray, Lord Jesus. Amen.

Starting university

Heavenly Father, I thank you for this great opportunity you have given me to study at uni. I thank you that you opened up the way for me to go there.

I acknowledge you, Lord God, as the One who has given me abilities and skills. In these coming years, heavenly Father, I pray that you will increase these skills and develop these abilities as I learn more. Be with those who teach me and who look after us all.

I pray, too, heavenly Father, that you will teach me about life. I pray that I may make good friends and we will have fun together, enjoying one another's company as we live for you in this, your world. Guard my life and protect me – and also use me to live for you and tell others about you, Lord Jesus.

I pray that the way I lead my life will be consistent with the words I speak. Develop my character so that I become even more like Christ. Give me wholeness, Lord: purity in heart, mind, body and will.

Help me with my finances, too, Lord. May I not waste the resources I have, but use money wisely.

Lord, I commit myself again to you today.

In Christ's name I pray. Amen.

Graduation

Lord, I can't really believe that my time at uni has now come to an end.

I want to thank you for all that I've learnt, the new experiences, new friends, new skills, whole new areas of learning and life you've opened up for me. I am so grateful for all the opportunities you have given me in these past years.

Thank you for being with me in all my studies, keeping me going through coursework, assignments, essays and exams, helping me with my finances, keeping me safe. Thank you for all those who have taught me and helped me in these past years.

Father, as the time comes now to enter the world of work, I pray for your guidance that soon I will find a good job where I can use the abilities and skills you've given me. Give me patience, heavenly Father, as I look for the right employment. May it not be too long before I find a job, I pray, heavenly Father.

In Christ's name. Amen.

New job

Heavenly Father, thank you for this new job you've given me. I acknowledge it has come about by you... how I saw the advertisement, applied, got the interview and was accepted... and now the big day has come!

Lord, as I meet new people, may I grasp quickly what my actual work involves. Help me as I face new challenges in applying my skills in a different environment.

I pray for your peace. Please still my racing heart. Please quieten my mind that has gone into overdrive.

I pray for my colleagues, that we will soon all get to know one another. May I remember all their names! May I settle down in this new job quickly, I pray, heavenly Father.

In Christ's name. Amen.

When your children have left home

So here we are, Lord: it's just us now; no noise, none of their music, none of their friends, none of their endless washing; none of their mess and untidiness: it's just us, Lord.

Is the nest – our home, *your* home – full or empty, Lord?

It may be empty of the children, who have lived in it for years, who have enjoyed it, used it – sometimes well, and sometimes not so well – but it's still full of you, Lord.

Lord, we know we can't keep our children under our protection for ever. Guide them in their work, with their friends, keep them safe and close to you; use them in this, your world. Help them as they leave, to cope with living on their own.

May we who are left, husband and wife, partners and heirs of eternal life, rediscover each other in greater depth. May we learn to enjoy each other's company more fully... May we recall why we fell in love with each other all those years ago.

Lord, we make ourselves available to you, put ourselves afresh at your disposal – for you to use us individually and together, as you will. In Jesus' name and for his sake, we pray. Amen.

Redundancy (see chapter 3, page 68)

Retirement

So the last day of work has finally come!

Lord God, I thank you for the gift of work – that you made us to serve you in this way. I thank you for the opportunity to honour you in this way over the years.

Now the time has come at last to rest from this work. Lord, may this time not be a rest from *all* work. May I continue to dream dreams and serve you in the years that lie ahead. Give me wisdom to know how to use the time and all the opportunities you give me, to get to know my grandchildren, to serve the church and the wider community... and to be ready for fresh adventures with you.

Lord, I welcome you into this new chapter in my life. May I face its challenges with your strength and your smile. I pray in Jesus' name. Amen.

Growing old

Lord, as the years tick by, I'm getting more and more anxious...

... about becoming dependent on others

... about losing my faculties

... because I may be left on my own with no one to look after me

... because I feel useless

... about missing out on my children growing up

... about financial difficulties

... about the unknown

... about dying.

Lord, help me, alongside my natural anxieties, to be thankful...

... for the years you have given me

... for my family and their love

... for close friends and their support

... for the experience and wisdom you have given me.

Lord, I do want to grow old gracefully... full of your grace, peace and hope. Lord Jesus, I want to know you more every day I live on this earth, until I see you face to face.

I pray this in your name, Lord Jesus. Amen.

3

Prayers in Times of Crisis

When death is near

As we walk through this valley, we come to you, Lord God.

In our sadness, may we know your comfort in our darkness, may we sense your presence in our bleakness, may we discover your hope in our anguish, may we find your strength.

Come and walk with us, Lord Jesus, we pray. May we know we are not alone: may you come alongside us on every step of our journey, even in this gloom.

Give us direction when we don't know which way to turn; give us courage when the path gets narrow and rocky; give us peace when the way becomes uncertain. Give us a glimpse of your hope, we pray, in Christ's name. Amen.

Funeral

On this day, Lord, we want to honour the life of our dear friend. Thank you for the years of life you gave them.

We thank you for their life, for all the gifts you gave them, for all that they achieved, and especially for the kind of people they were. Thank you for the good and happy times we shared.

We acknowledge you as the Giver of life.

We pray for your strength and comfort for those who mourn. Support them in their bereavement and deep sense of loss, when they walk through the valley of the shadow of death. Give them strength in their grief. May we do all we can to help them at this sad and difficult time.

When bereaved

I can't believe what has happened.

I feel completely numb.

To think, they were alive yesterday and now they have ... gone.

Help me, Lord, through this time.

May I know you're mourning with me in my tears, in my loss.

May I somehow sense your comfort and your presence.

Help me with all the practical things I need to sort out.

May I know you are with me in this awful valley of death.

On the unexpected death of a child

Lord, what's happened is so tragic. I can't believe it. They were here one day and gone the next.

Why, Lord? Why did they have to go? Why? Why? Why? Where are you, Lord? I thought you were all-powerful. Why didn't you stop them from dying?

I pray that somehow you will bring light into our present darkness. I pray for you to comfort us in our shock and complete disbelief. I pray for your power and strength in our numbness. Please give us some hope at this terrible time. In Christ's name we pray. Amen.

When your partner has died

Lord, I feel completely devastated, terrible and in despair right now. I'm in shock, totally bewildered, and can't believe what has happened. Help me in my desperate state, in my loneliness and grief. Help me to come to terms with what has happened.

I can still hear their voice, their footsteps; I can still sense their presence but the fact that they aren't here any more has still to sink in.

I don't feel like doing any of the practical things I've got to do... making arrangements for the funeral, tidying up their affairs and so on.

I just feel so awful and pray for your help. May I not put on a false face that I'm coping. If people want to know how I'm really feeling, may I be brave and tell them.

May I accept the comfort and support of family and friends. Come and wrap your loving arms around me at this time. Please help me. Please give me the strength and courage to get through today. Amen.

Breaking up of a relationship

Lord, the pain is so devastating, the anger so bitter. Our friendship, our love, our trust have all come to such an abrupt end. I feel I'm all at sea, I'm left clinging to a broken piece of timber heading for a waterfall. My life has been completely torn apart and I don't know what to do.

Help me find a measure of calm soon, Lord, I pray that I may be able to make decisions about my future. At the moment everything seems completely bleak, but I pray that you will give me some fresh light, hope and courage.

When your partner has walked out on you

Lord, I just can't believe what has happened. How could it have come to this? I thought we were so happy together... our life was all mapped out, all our hopes and dreams... and now everything is in pieces.

Perhaps I should have seen the warning signs, but I didn't, or I didn't face up to them. Please help me, Lord. I don't know which way to turn right now.

Thank you for friends who I know will stand by me at this terrible time. Help me to sort my life out. Help me to be able to trust people again in the not-too-distant future, Lord, I pray. Amen.

Divorce

Lord, all our dreams are shattered. I never thought it would come to this. How could it have happened to us? We've reached the end of the road.

Lord, I come to you at this time... confused, bewildered, deeply hurt and fragile inside. I pray for your help right now, especially for the children, that you will guide us through this mess.

I thank you, Lord, that you are still Lord of my life. I pray for friends to guide and support me during this terrible time as I try to rebuild my life.

Please help me, Lord, I pray. Amen.

Breakdown

I'm not sure I can continue, Lord. I feel I'm coming to the end of myself in so many ways.

Spiritually, Lord, I am not really sure of your presence any more. *Emotionally*, Lord, I feel drained – as I've been running on empty for a long time. *Physically*, Lord, I feel totally worn out and hardly able to do anything. Please help. I feel I'm about to fall apart completely.

And yet, Lord, I am still praying to you. Please come to me and rescue me. Thank you for friends and family who mean well – even if their offers of help aren't really what I need.

I really am desperate, Lord. I cry out to you from the depths of my being that you will come and help me at this time in my life. Please, Lord, come and bring a ray of hope into my life right now. May I somehow come to know that I am not completely on my own in this situation and that some change – even a small one, please, Lord – is possible.

I pray in Jesus' name. Amen.

In a mid-life crisis

Lord, I feel such a sense of failure. As I look back over the years, I wonder where they have all gone, as time has slipped by so quickly.

Nothing seems to mean much any more. I have no sense of achievement. I have lost all sense of adventure in life. The children have flown the nest. I feel I'm just existing, going through the motions of life, not really living any more.

I see how we tried to bring up our children. I know I can get too easily caught up in what went wrong.

Help me not to focus so much on the past, what I have lost, but to remember you are Lord of all – of my life, of the future, of everything.

Lord, I don't know really where I'm going! Please help me to refocus on my destination, *then* I'll know where my life is going.

Help me to feel the touch of your love, find new direction, a more focused hope for my journey, a fresh sense of adventure, I pray.

When you have been made redundant

Lord, I can't believe this has happened. We kind of knew the company was in financial difficulties but never thought it would come to this.

Lord, please help us. We're going to need wisdom, your practical guidance on what to do... how to make ends meet, how to manage, to see if we need to move to find another job, all sorts of things.

May we not be too proud to ask others to help.

Please may we know your peace and your presence at this difficult time.

When you find out your child is on drugs

Why did they do it, Lord?

We're absolutely devastated right now. Where did we go wrong? What did we fail in?

How could they be so stupid? After all we've taught them, tried to guide and show them through the years, and now... this...

Lord, guide us as to what to do, what to say... and what *not* to say... how to react, how to help.

We cry out to you for hope even in this desperate situation. May we not give up on our children, because you do not.

Thank you for others who are with us, friends to support us and to pray for us. May we all help our child through this time to grow to become the person you intend them to be.

When you feel like committing suicide

Lord, all hope has gone and I'm desperate.

I feel trapped by my circumstances. Life seems completely meaningless. I cannot see a way out.

O God, if you are there, please redirect my thought life from what is negative or destructive. Please protect me from causing myself harm or injury.

Please give me courage and strength to face each day. Show me there is a way forward.

Give me the courage to admit I need help, and to contact the people who can help me.

I feel such a failure, that my life is not worth anything, and that no one would miss me if I wasn't here.

I've got no one to share my deepest, innermost thoughts with.

Relieve the desperate turmoil and anguish I feel.

(See www.samaritans.org. Tel. 08457 90 90 90)

In times of war

Lord, I sense my enemies are all around me and may attack me at any time. Devastation and maybe even death may come.

Lord, I turn to you in this crisis. May I not be completely gripped by fear, but may I depend on you to give me courage to overcome my natural fears.

Stop the forces of evil from gaining victory. May the horror and suffering of war come to an end soon. May peace, harmony and justice come quickly. May the cause of right prevail. May I stand up for what I believe in as a Christian. Lord, you promised that at such times you would give your people the words to say and I cry out to you now to enable me to speak for you.

May I help others who don't know you – may my life and my words point them to you.

But in some ways, Lord, the time for mere words is over and we are in a life-and-death situation. I cry out to you for mercy. I have no confidence at all in myself; all my confidence is in you.

Help me not to despair but to trust in you. May I suffer with courage and cheerfulness. May I remain faithful to you.

I freely confess my sins; I acknowledge you as my Lord and Saviour.

Be merciful to me, my family and loved ones. I pray for your protection. Guard me; keep me and my loved ones safe and secure. May I even love my enemies, with your help.

Lord, may your kingdom come. May I see Christ himself coming soon. I give my life to you afresh right now. Amen.

When your pet has died

Lord God and Father of all, I thank you for the gift of life you gave my friend and companion. I thank you that you know how much I am missing them. I know you understand my loss, pain and sense of bereavement now that they have gone.

Thank you for their liveliness and brightness, and for their company. Thank you for the memories I have and for the many years of happiness my friend brought me.

If there were a heaven for pets, I believe my friend would be there now.

Please comfort me in my loss. Amen.

4

Prayers in Good Times

Thanking God

Heavenly Father, I want to express my thankfulness to you for life, for breath, for good friends, for my family, job and home. I acknowledge that all these are gifts from your hand. Forgive me that I take them for granted so much. You are so good!

I thank you most of all for Jesus Christ, my Saviour and Lord. I thank you for his closeness, for his love, for his standing by me through the good times, the bad times and just the ordinary times... and even when I fail. I thank you that you don't give up on me.

I thank you that Christ died on the cross for me to take away my sin, to bring me back home to yourself, to put me in a right relationship with you so that I could come to know you as one of your children.

I thank you for the Bible, your written word, that it points so clearly to Christ.

I thank you for the deep sense of assurance you give me that I know Jesus Christ personally.

Lord, I do appreciate all that you are and have done. I pray that my whole life will be an expression of gratitude to you, through Jesus Christ, I pray. Amen.

Thanksgiving for God's creation

Heavenly Father, I stand in awe at the majesty of your creation. To think that you are my God and Master and that I know you!

When I stop to ponder all that you have made, my heart rises in adoration, worship, and praise.

I worship you, Lord God, for the splendour and magnificence of all you have made – the vast expanse of the desert, the bold depths of the ocean, the grandeur of mountain ranges ... right down to velvety rose petals and the tiny fingernails of a newborn baby.

Lord, your whole creation is fearfully and wonderfully made!

I worship you in Jesus' name. Amen.

When you feel joyful

Heavenly Father, I worship you that I am full of joy at this time.

I celebrate your goodness, Father. I praise you...

... for your care, in providing all I need, in looking after me in difficult times

... for creation, that Lord God, you make all things

... for salvation in Christ, that I know Jesus Christ as my personal Saviour

... for the gift of faith, that as I turn to you and trust you, I know peace with God

... for your word, the Bible, through which you speak to me so clearly

... for my friends and family, with whom I can share so much

... for the church that I am part of, that I can join my brothers and sisters in praising you

... for the world you have put me in, that I can enjoy the good gifts you lavish on me so generously.

Living God – Father, Son and Spirit – I adore you in worship.

When you feel worshipful

Lord God, we declare your goodness. You are great and worthy of all praise and adoration. You created all things. You are to be honoured and worshipped. You are eternal, awesome and majestic. How beautiful and dazzling you must be!

We exalt you because you are holy, good and faithful. We praise you because you are love: you are rich in mercy and full of grace.

As we come to you in reverence, Lord God, we see our complete unworthiness to step into your divine pure presence. We are amazed that you should bother with us at all. We acknowledge we have defied your holiness and broken your laws. We have wanted to go our own way. We confess our sins. Forgive us and cleanse us for these wrongs. Purify our hearts afresh, we pray.

May we show our gratitude for your forgiveness by leading lives of service, giving ourselves humbly and willingly to serve others in need. Come and show us yourself more and more. Come and shine in our hearts even more brightly through Jesus Christ. In his name we pray. Amen.

When you feel close to God

O living God, I worship you and love you. I thank you for the wonderful privilege of knowing you through Jesus Christ. I thank you that I sense your closeness to me right now. I can almost reach out and touch you. I sense your intimate nearness. I can come right into your presence. I am so thrilled with joy in you! I worship you in the warmth of your presence.

I worship you for forgiveness through your Son, my precious Saviour, Jesus Christ. I *know* that Christ died for *me*, that I am *completely forgiven*, that I am a child of God!

You give me your power and blessings. I thank you for refreshing me with your love. I want to bask in the light of your glory for ever. May I continue to enjoy you, I pray, in Jesus' name. Amen.

When you are prayerful

I thank you, heavenly Father, that you have given us hearts to seek you, hearts that long for you. We recognize that all we have and are comes from you. You are our God and Father; you are the living God.

Thank you for giving us a deep trust and confidence in you.

Convict us afresh of our sins, turn us deeply back to Christ that we may be completely cleansed.

We acknowledge that we are sinners, but we worship you that you have not left us in our sins but have come to us in Christ to forgive us, to purify us, and to bring us home to yourself.

We thank you that you slow down the pace of our lives, and you quieten our spirits to listen to you.

Lord, as we meditate on your word, share your heart with us and show us again what you are like. We want to honour your name. Enlarge our view of your greatness; stir up in us a deeper and warmer devotion to you.

Set us alight to declare the glory of God and the message of Christ. Pour out your grace and mercy, your light and life, into us so that we will bring hope to individuals and whole communities.

Lord, save us from wanting this experience for ourselves. You want to reach out through us into this dry world. May the fresh life-giving streams of your living water flow out from us into where we live and work.

Make us more deeply aware of people's spiritual needs. Work in our offices and canteens, in our schools, our colleges and universities. Work in Parliament and in national and regional assemblies, in our town halls, hospitals, prisons, in our supermarkets and shopping malls, in our banks and insurance offices, in our factories and on our oil rigs, in our buses and trains, in the newspapers and TV stations.

May your will be done on earth. In Jesus' name. Amen.

Desiring God

Lord, we long to be closer to you, to know you even more intimately. Our greatest desire is to deepen our friendship with you, to experience more of the unfathomable riches of Christ.

Help us to slow down again, to meditate on you, your word and your love. May we taste again of your love. Holy Spirit, come as the dew to refresh us with your sweet touch as we focus our lives again on Christ.

May our love for you be genuine, Lord, not pretend. Show us anything that is preventing us from getting to know you more; anything that is stopping us from deepening our relationship with you.

May we be less concerned about our own ease and comfort and more concerned to become like our Lord and Saviour, Jesus Christ.

May our passion for you, Lord, be rekindled. Fan into flame the embers of our devotion for you. Amen.

5

Prayers for Other People

For children and young people

Lord Jesus, we remember how you welcomed children into your presence. You told us we were to become as humble as children to receive your kingdom.

Thank you for the children and young people you give us. We pray for their *safety*, Lord, in this world. There are so many dangers – some hidden, some open. Please keep them secure in the love of their families, friends, church and in the wider communities. Please stop the forces of evil from harming these little ones.

We pray for their *salvation*, Lord, that they would come to know

Jesus Christ as their own personal Saviour at an early age. We pray their trust in Christ will mature as they grow up, and that they will know he is Lord of every aspect of their lives. We pray for those who teach children and young people, that you will keep them from misusing their positions of trust, and that they will not only teach wisely but also be good examples of character and integrity to those they are responsible for.

Lord, give our children and young people good health, good friends and good desires. Give them the strength to overcome difficulties and to learn from them. May they quickly learn to have confidence in themselves, developing the personality and character you have given them. May they learn to take responsibility at an early age. Give them times of fun and play. May they develop a sense of humour and keep a sense of adventure throughout their whole lives.

In Jesus' name we pray. Amen.

For the activity of the church

Lord Jesus, you promised that you would be with your people when they meet together. We claim that promise right now.

We know that you are with us, but even so, Lord, we pray that you will give us a sense of your presence all together and individually, that we may have a fresh experience of the living God.

We worship you for rescuing us from death and condemnation, for giving us Christ, for life, peace, and your eternal love.

May we hear your voice speaking clearly to us today.

Make us more sensitive to you, and to the awfulness of turning away from you.

Lead us into a deeper joy as we look to you.

Bring life to your people; purify your church, cleanse us from our sin as we turn back to you; revive us spiritually. Renew us, not so that we become even busier people, at church still more evenings in the week, but so that we become more involved with people in our community.

Spirit of God, give us a burden for souls, Lord, souls who, without you, are perishing.

Lord, we pray for the church, your people, that we will truly become the people you intend us to be, that we will really look upward to you, and that we will look outward to others, not simply look to ourselves.

Lord, make us a distinctive people, to bring you our praise, worship and adoration, and to lead lives of godly consistency and integrity.

May we all pull together, working as one strong and resilient team, to bring you a symphony of worship and praise, and to take you to the community and the wider world.

May our energies be clearly focused and our lives inspired and directed by your power at this time.

We pray in Christ's name. Amen.

For church leaders

Father God, we pray for those who lead the church. We thank you for them. We thank you that you have called them to this task, to be shepherds of the flock. Thank you for the faith you have given them.

We pray that you will guide them and equip them. As they wait on you, may you speak to them together through the word and Spirit, to lead them clearly into the purposes you have for us all.

May they be godly men and women whose lives are simply like Christ himself.

May they have courage to make difficult decisions.

Deepen their trust in you. Breathe your life into them afresh.

May our leaders teach us wisely. Give those who declare your word such power, fervency and boldness that can only come from you. Revive our confidence in your word, the Bible. Renew us – refresh us spiritually; may we return to your word and to truly godly living. Give us humble, sensitive, tender, responsive hearts. Make us stable and strong for you. Remove any critical, negative spirit in us. Convict us of our habitual sins.

Lord, where necessary, please unsettle us all to see the holy urgency of the tasks that face us. May you lead us all to have an impact on society in this generation.

Make us all more wholly yours. Fill us all again with your Spirit. May we all know you, Father, Son and Spirit, more and more... May we submit more fully to you. May we know a fuller power in prayer, a closer friendship with you.

Make us more sensitive to your holiness, more aware of our inner sin, and then more like Christ himself. May our souls remain thirsty, and our prayers continue to be urgent, that we may build up a spiritual storehouse of godly power through your Spirit that we may draw on at the appointed time. Electrify us all with your power. May we not set any limits on how you may work, but simply allow you to be God in our midst. Enlarge our vision to realize afresh how you can work more widely and more deeply than we could imagine in our wildest dreams, more than we could ever think possible.

In Jesus' name we pray. Amen.

For the mission of the church

Lord, open our eyes to see the task of going in Christ's name into your world with the good news of Jesus Christ.

We acknowledge again that we depend on you to give us what we need to sustain us on our journey through life. Make us more intimate in knowing Christ. May we fall in love with him again.

Release us to share our faith boldly, naturally and spontaneously. Re-energize us in our praise and worship of the living God.

May we learn afresh to serve one another in true love and to be bold in bringing the goodness of Jesus Christ to a needy world.

In some places, Lord, the ground is barren. May we sow with faith, watering and nurturing the seeds of your word with prayer and sensitivity.

In many other places, Lord, the fields are ready to be harvested. May we go faithfully, boldly and in the power of your Spirit to gather in newcomers to follow Jesus Christ.

Lord of the harvest, we pray that you will send out workers into your fields.

Give us a renewed confidence in the gospel of Christ, that it really *is* the power of God to save men, women and young

people who at present do not know you. We thank you again for the power of the cross of Christ.

Work in our lives individually and together so that you can use us. Mould us, equip us to bring the living water of Christ to a dry and needy community, to bring a fresh touch of your Spirit to those around us.

Baptize us with your Spirit to make us strong and bold.

Give us a heightened sense of urgency to live for Christ today where we are now, and to speak out for you as opportunities open up for us.

Stir up in us an even deeper desire to pray. Set our hearts on fire to seek you and to pray for our world.

May we all go out, trusting you, with your authority, living and declaring the incredible life-changing good news of Jesus Christ, for we pray this in his name. Amen.

For the persecuted church

Lord, your word tells us to remember those in prison as if we were with them there. We transport ourselves to a dark, hot, filthy cell to be with our brothers and sisters in Christ.

Forgive us, Lord, for our comfort, ease and complacency, for how we grumble and complain at the slightest difficulty we encounter. Our brothers and sisters in Christ who are being persecuted for trusting you put us to shame.

94

Give them hope, strength and courage when they are tempted to give up. Support them and their families in their isolation.

May you, Lord Jesus Christ, make yourself known even more deeply both to them and to us, for we pray this in your name. Amen.

For the unity of the church

Heavenly Father, your church is so precious to you. You must grieve as you see our divisions and our warring factions.

We pray that we might be truly as one, as you are, Holy Trinity: Father, Son and Spirit. May your Holy Spirit lead us into all truth, as we sincerely follow your word and as we truly worship our Lord Jesus Christ.

May we not break the unity you give us by our pride, jealousy and selfishness, but may we rightly and lovingly affirm one another's gifts and callings, that those outside the church may come to know Jesus Christ and put their trust in him.

We pray in his name. Amen.

For our community

I thank you, heavenly Father, for all those who work in our community to make things go smoothly.

For those in *schools*: the head teacher, teachers, assistants and helpers, governors, caretaker, cleaners; in *hospitals*: doctors, consultants, nurses, administrators, technical staff and cleaners.

For those who work for the *police, ambulance service* and *fire and rescue service*, for *shopkeepers* – for those who serve and stock the *shops* and *supermarkets*; for those who work in the *garages* and *filling stations*; for *postmen* and *postwomen*; *farmers* and those who *deliver milk*; those who work in *hotels* and *cafés*.

Lord, I'm sure I've missed out some; forgive me. Thank you for the hard work all these people do, day in, day out... usually unnoticed.

May I show my appreciation to more of these people I have mentioned, I pray, Lord, to encourage them in their routine tasks and jobs. In Jesus' name I pray. Amen.

For our country

Lord, you see how much our country has turned away from you. We are like a dry, barren desert, largely lacking in spiritual life.

Come, Lord, refresh us again with the water of your Spirit. May Jesus Christ be worshipped truly. May your word again be honoured and revered.

May people turn to you and come to know you not only as their creator, but also as their Lord and Saviour.

We pray for all those who lead us, in local and national politics, in our armed forces and emergency services, in our schools, colleges and universities, in our media – television, radio, newspapers and computer networks.

We long for your voice to be made known more clearly, your will and purposes to be declared more fully, your values to be upheld more firmly.

Strengthen your church, heavenly Father; draw your people back to seek you in humble prayer. Lead us to confess our sins before you more freely and deeply, and to turn away from all that is not right. Mould us, prepare us and equip us to fulfil all that you want us to be, to worship you more sincerely and to serve the fellow members of our communities more wholeheartedly.

In Christ's name. Amen.

For the environment

Heavenly Father, this is your world. You are Lord of all of it. Everything in it belongs to you.

Forgive us that we have abused your goodness.

Forgive us that we have wasted resources.

Forgive us that we have polluted the environment around us.

Lord, if it is not too late, help each one of us to do what we can to save our planet, *your* planet.

May we learn to be good managers of *everything* you have given us, to be far less wasteful in our industry and homes, in the way we live and work.

We pray this in the name of the Saviour of the world, Jesus Christ. Amen.

For the homeless

Lord Jesus Christ, you know what it was like not to have a home. You had no home of your own.

Look with mercy, we pray, on those who have no home of their own.

And may those who have good homes not only say the right words, but also do something active and positive to help those in need in this way.

Instead of coldness, may there be warmth.

Instead of loneliness, may there be friendship.

Instead of isolation, may there be an affirmed place in the community.

May your people, we pray, be in the forefront of serving others in this way.

In Christ's name. Amen.

For those who are ill

Lord God, great healer of all, I pray right now for friends who are ill or who are being treated in hospital. Please give the nurses and doctors wisdom in knowing how best to help our friends get better.

Please give your courage in suffering; give your comfort in pain; give your strength in weakness; give your hope in uncertainty.

Please come near to family and friends to help them through this very difficult time. We pray in Jesus' name. Amen.

For those who are mentally ill

Lord God, we come to you as we pray for our friend. We thank you that you deal gently and tenderly with us all.

Please restore their whole being; please bring your hope in the face of despair; please give your courage alongside the sense that nothing will ever change; please bring the spark of your light in the face of nothingness.

We trust you as we pray for our friend. In Jesus' precious name. Amen.

For justice in the world

Lord God, you who are the God of truth, love and justice. We pray that we will see that truth, love and justice established in our own society in this generation.

Lord God, challenge our comforts, rebuke our ease and laziness. Disturb us that we do not remain unmoved at so much human suffering. May we not only sit up and take notice, but also stir ourselves to action to serve you.

Give us the eyes of Christ to see those in need, the homeless, the downtrodden and the exploited. Give us the heart of Christ to be moved by compassion, pity and love. Give us the hands of Christ to help bring peace into this world of conflict, to hold the hands of those who are broken, to love those who are unlovely, to cherish and nurture the image of God in every human soul.

In Christ's name and for his sake we pray. Amen.

For your neighbours

I thank you for my neighbours, Father. I thank you for their kind acts; in bringing in the post and deliveries when I'm out, in keeping an eye on my home when I'm away.

In the middle of all the friendly banter, may something of my natural humanity be evident in the ordinary routines of life.

Lord, if there are opportunities to especially help my neighbours – or to get to know them more deeply – then may I not be afraid to grasp them, for your sake.

May I be sensitive to what is going on around me; being kind, listening to others and speaking words of encouragement to those in my community.

Lord, I pray for the new folks who've just moved in. May I be welcoming to them – not too in-your-face welcoming! – but showing them due respect.

Lord, may your kingdom come in my neighbourhood.

It would be fantastic, Lord, if most people – or even if more people – where I live truly came to know you and love you. Soften people's hearts towards you.

In Christ's name I pray. Amen.

For peace

Your word says that you are the Prince of Peace and that there will be no end to the increase of your government and peace.

Lord, is time running out to make peace?

Lord, is there a limit to your rule and to your peace? Surely not.

And yet in my mind's eye I can see it now.

Hospitals wrongly bombed.

Helpless, powerless lives lost.

Innocent people dying.

But these are people, Lord, just like *my* wife/husband, *my* children, people with names, people with identities.

Lord, bring peace, I ask, in this, your world.

May I, too, not simply pray for peace, but may I also be a peacemaker, doing what I can, where you have put me, to serve you to bring peace where I live and work. I pray in the name of the Prince of Peace. Amen.

For those in prison

Lord, I pray for my friend who is in prison. Help me to see them through your eyes, to bring acceptance instead of condemnation, love instead of hatred, and affirmation instead of worthlessness.

I pray that my friend will grow through their experience in prison at this time; that they will grow in their respect for themselves and for others. May this time draw them closer to you, too, I pray.

I pray also for members of their family, that you will be with them at this difficult time, and that they will know your presence in their loneliness.

I pray that the prison officers and staff will be good role models and encouragers. May my friend make good friendships with other inmates. May the prison governor and those with responsibility for running the prison do so justly and fairly.

I bring my dear friend before you right now, in Jesus' name. Amen.

For refugees and asylum seekers

Lord God, you call your people to care for people from other countries in our community. We pray for those who have had to leave their own homes, families and countries.

We pray for those who seek asylum in our country that they will be kept safe, have their basic needs met, and be treated fairly. Lord God, you know the feelings of powerlessness, frustration and bewilderment, the sense that their life is 'in limbo' at the moment. May decisions on their future not be delayed unduly.

We pray for those who have been granted permanent visas, that they will settle down in our own community, find work and make good friendships; that they will discover your plan for their lives. May they know hope and courage as they face the future. Amen.

Why do so many resist you?

Lord, why do so many people seem to resist your word? I am sad that so many seem to be insensitive to spiritual matters.

Why don't they acknowledge you instead of defying you? Why can't they see you made the world and everything in it? Why won't they recognize you?

Help me to share Christ with these, my friends and members of my family as tenderly as I can, seeking a response in them.

May I continue to take care of them and love them whether they want to have anything to do with you or not.

Lord Jesus, give me your strength, your endurance, your patience, your perseverance to be there for them always.

Soften their hearts, Lord, I pray, to receive you soon. Amen.

For revival

Lord, look from heaven, from your glory and your holiness. Look on us in your love, mercy and power. We pray that you will move and come from your home of glory to touch this earth afresh.

Convict us of our sin; may we repent deeply from our hearts. Forgive us that we have pandered to the flesh, we have not called sin 'sin' but have soft-pedalled it, playing it down. May we have your view of sin, considering it as serious and that it offends you in your holiness. Forgive our indifference and unbelief, our unwillingness, reluctance and distrust. Jolt us out of our complacency and preoccupation with ourselves.

May we be humble and penitent, prayerful and expectant; may we be completely open to you, willing to change and be changed. May the fresh wind of your reviving break us, mould us and fill us again. May we become even more obedient to, more centred on, your will.

In those areas of our lives where we are still holding out against you, even to a small extent, please may we truly accept your Lordship, to make us more like the Lord Jesus Christ himself.

We are wandering through the wilderness of life; we desperately need you to pour out your Holy Spirit to wake us all up to reality.

Bring life to your people; purify your church, cleanse us from our sin as we turn back to you; revive us spiritually. Refine us and purify us. Set our hearts alight again with your fire.

Demonstrate, even in our time, even today – even now! – the victory Jesus Christ won at Calvary. May we enter into all the fullness of the joy of the Lord that is rightfully ours.

Feed us spiritually from your word. May we use the Bible – the sword of the Spirit – in our warfare. Reduce our caution and fears. Increase our love for your word and your world.

Break into our lives – *my* life – with your power. Bring healing to those parts that are broken or out of joint.

Lord Jesus, show your resurrection power among us. Reveal yourself 'outside the box' of the conventional ways in which we think you might work. Break through the boundaries we have set on your activity. Surprise us with your activity, Lord; do something unexpected among us. Lord, we plead with you to do something amazing and extraordinary among us.

We pray right now for unsaved members of our families, friends who are at this moment eternally lost, our neighbours, our colleagues at work. We pray they would all know Jesus Christ personally.

May we not settle for less, may we continue to seek you and not be satisfied with anything less than a deeper revelation and experience of yourself.

May your revival not be limited to the church, but may you also open the eyes of those who do not know you, and heal the hearts of those at present in Satan's power.

Challenge our culture; energize us to bring renewal and reform to our tired society and nation.

Lord, the nations of the world need you; this country needs you; our community needs you.

May your people serve the local communities you have put us in with renewed zeal. May you work through us to bring peace, justice and reconciliation to those who know only conflict, and who are powerless, and who do not know you.

So we, Lord, want more of you. May your kingdom come, even in our generation, even through *us*, even through *me.*

Lord, keep us praying for revival until you answer our prayers. In Jesus' name. Amen.

For those with special needs

Heavenly Father, you created each person on this planet as individuals. You made us all to be different.

We thank you for these differences that are so much part of who we are. May we remember that every single one of us is special to you, that we are each fearfully, wonderfully and distinctively made in your image. May we therefore honour and respect each other, realizing we all need one another to express our common humanity.

We thank you that your grace is not something that is earned or that depends on our abilities; it is simply given to each one of us as a gift.

May we respect and honour one another more deeply. May we learn how we can love, affirm and encourage one another more meaningfully so that we may all grow closer to you and each other.

In Jesus' name we pray. Amen.

Spiritual warfare

112

Almighty God, we thank you for the victory the Lord Jesus Christ won on the cross over Satan. We want to live in the power of that victory even today. Advance the cause of good. Restrain the forces that oppose your purposes. May we constantly remember that the victory over the world, the flesh and the devil has already been won.

May you yourself continually be our vision that we may trust in you fully to see us through, not depending on our own strength. May we stand firm in all your spiritual resources, may our minds be set on you and your grace, may our righteousness be fully assured in Christ, and may we be ready to serve you as we live and speak for you, constantly taking in your word and praying to you.

We do not want to lead lives that are constantly defeated – your word declares that we are more than conquerors through Christ, and we pray for that to become true in our own lives even now.

We pray, too, for our wider community and nation, that you will release the unlimited power of Christ over spiritual forces that at present bind people, that you will right now turn around situations we currently consider hopeless.

Demonstrate that you are Lord of all the world. Drive back areas of darkness. Bring healing where there is sickness and disease.

May we all become strong – and remain strong – in you and your power. We pray all these things on the basis of the authority of our Lord Jesus Christ. Amen.

For the unemployed

Heavenly Father, part of your will is that we should work to serve you and those around us.

Give hope and creativity where there is anger, frustration and a sense of hopelessness. Grant that those who are now unemployed may soon be able to find a job that not only provides financial resources, but also gives joy and fulfilment. May their skills not go to waste; please give practical guidance, I pray in Christ's name. Amen.

For those who have been victims of abuse or war

Lord, I want to pray for my friends who have suffered so terribly. I cannot begin to enter into the pain they go through and are still suffering.

I pray, Lord Jesus, that somehow they will know your presence in the memories of their terror, your courage and comfort in their pain, your healing in their wounds and your hope as they try to rebuild their lives. Give them the strength and power they need at this very difficult time.

I pray that I will be a true friend who will be with them; who will, at the right time, listen to them with your love, acceptance and compassion. In Jesus' name. Amen.

Anger at events going on in the world

Lord, I'm angry at all the pain in the world, the injustice, the brutalities, the inhumanity of one person to another, when everyone was originally made in your image.

Lord, if I feel this way – how must you feel toward it?

May I serve you where I can today, right now in the community where I live and work.

May I play my part to see wrongs put right, to see your kingdom come.

May I treat with respect everyone I meet, speak to on the phone, email or send text messages to. May I remember that each one of us was originally made in your image.

May your righteous kingdom come a little more, even today, Lord. May your will be done even on earth, where I live, in my life and in the lives of those close to me.

I pray in Christ's name. Amen.

For the world

Heavenly Father, we pray for peace in this, your world. We pray for your kingdom to come, your will to be done. We pray for your glory to be made known in the world, that more and more people will come to acknowledge Jesus Christ as their Lord and Saviour. May we all come to know him more deeply, we pray.

We ask, Lord, too, that people in authority throughout the world will make wise and just decisions – ones based on others' needs and thoughts rather than from selfish motives.

Restrain the power of evil, subdue the powers of darkness; make effective and prosper the work of sharing the good news of Jesus Christ as we live for you today.

In Christ's name we pray. Amen.

6

Prayers in Everyday Life

The everyday

Lord, as I go about today's ordinary duties and routines may I be aware of you.

There isn't the slightest shadow of darkness in you, O Lord. You are completely pure and right. So may my life reflect more and more what you are like in the way I really live.

Give me eyes to notice you in everything: the vastness of your creation, the beauty of a shiny leaf; may I be sensitive to the subtle delights of life around me – a smile, a wave, a listening ear.

I know I fail so often, but I thank you again that I may know the fresh assurance of the blood of Christ cleansing me from every wrong. Thank you, Jesus, for being my Saviour and Lord.

Help me somehow – with your strength, Lord – to rise above the frustrations and inconveniences that I know I will experience today.

Save me from being dulled by the repetitiveness of life. May I respond to the rich texture of life in the community where I live and work. May I appreciate the wide diversity of cultures around me.

May my life have integrity – that consistency and wholeness between what I say I believe and how I actually live in practice. May I live in your reality today.

Lord, I don't simply want to survive today, just to get through it. Your word promises life in all its fullness. May I welcome each new moment with expectant and obedient delight to be ready to serve you and others. May I know that today, as I find even deeper meaning, purpose and values... as I seek you – and find you – afresh. I pray in Jesus' name. Amen.

Morning (1)

Lord, the last thing I want to do is get out of bed this morning.

I want to go back under the duvet and stay there all day.

I don't think I can face the day ahead.

Please give me the strength and courage just to take things one moment at a time.

Help me to cope with everything that happens, and may I sense your presence with me.

Lord Jesus, in your name I pray. Amen.

Morning (2)

Thank you, Lord, for this new day.

Thank you for its freshness – for the birds I can hear singing, the dawn chorus to your majesty and greatness.

I feel excited about all the possibilities this new day has to offer, this fresh start, the work I will do, the people I will meet.

Lord, I pray that I may not have too much hassle getting the children ready for school, getting to and from work, thinking of ways to keep the kids occupied, knowing what to cook this evening. Lord, I pray that most things will go smoothly... please, Lord!

May I live in your strength, moment by moment, depending on you. May I learn to follow you more closely, not repeating the mistakes of yesterday.

Help me to rise above the ordinary. Lord, your word says that we are more than conquerors through Christ. I don't just want to get through today; I want to know your power to live a life that counts, one that is effective.

Keep me safe and near to you. In Christ's name I pray. Amen.

Morning (3)

I greet the present moment with joyful delight, expectant hope and ready obedience.

This day is yours and I commit myself afresh to you.

My heart is ready to sing your praises! O my soul, wake me up fully. May I lift up my heart to you. May my whole being, the depths of my heart, worship and adore you!

You are God, Lord. You are a faithful God, and I trust you with the details of the day. You are a sovereign God and may I remember that you are in control whatever happens today.

You are a righteous God and I pray that justice and right will come, and be seen to come, in this, your world even this day.

Morning (4)

Lord, my to-do list is already bulging at the seams. Where do I begin?

I'm overwhelmed even before I begin to tackle the tasks before me.

Lord, may I not lose sight of people as I work through all I have to do... real people, with thoughts and feelings just like me. May I somehow – with your strength! – honour them.

And, Lord, may I not forget you in all my busyness. Please sustain me.

I acknowledge again that apart from you I can do nothing, but I know, too, that with you I can do all things.

Give me the energy I need to cope with all that will come my way. I depend on Christ right now. Amen.

At night (1)

Father, I have come to the end of another day. As I look back over it, I realize there are

... some things I should not have done

... some things I should not have said

... some things I should not have thought.

I confess, too, that I have not done what I have known to be right or true.

I am sorry that you, Lord Jesus, have not been uppermost in my life this day.

I ask again for your forgiveness, that I may know your cleansing.

Thank you that you give sleep to those who are dear to you. I pray for a good night's refreshment and rest. I affirm my trust in you again. In Jesus' name. Amen.

At night (2)

Father God, I thank you that you have looked after me today. I thank you that you have provided for me today. You have given me clothes, shelter, money, a job, family and friends.

I acknowledge that all these are gifts that have come from your hand. I thank you for your goodness towards your whole creation. I pray for peace in your world.

As I go to rest now Father, I thank you for the gift of sleep. I pray that I will know your rest and restoration within me, that I will awake alert and ready to serve you tomorrow. Amen.

At night (3)

Lord, you know I'm completely exhausted right now. I am so tired I can hardly put my words together. Thank you for the promise of sleep... the gift of sleep you give to your dear ones.

Help me to sleep soundly without interruption and to awake refreshed, with the vision and the energy you give to face a new day.

Lord, I do want to affirm again my trust in you. May I know that I can truly do everything with your strength actively working inside me. It would be wonderful to be able to say that the joy of the Lord is my strength – to be able to say that and really mean it.

Ordinary days

Lord, it looks as if today will be just another ordinary day. Things will probably tick over nicely, with no major ups and downs, with nothing unexpected.

But Lord, I pray that you will break into the sheer ordinariness with your touch, your light, your life.

Lord, surprise me with a fresh assurance of your presence even today.

Sustain me in my spirit. Renew within me a sense of life as an adventure with you, I pray. In Jesus' name. Amen.

Everyday conversations

Lord, make me a person who will listen sensitively to people around me today rather than always jumping straight in and talking.

May I really listen to people... listen... listen... listen. Lord, that's hard work. May I be genuinely interested in others, more concerned for them than for me to have my say.

May I give words of encouragement. May my conversation be gracious. May my words have a truly human, even prophetic, edge to them, without my being aware of it.

Lord, speak through me today, I pray. Amen.

When your computer goes wrong

Lord, it's done it again, I don't know what's wrong with it. But you understand all about bytes, silicon chips, circuit, broadband and the Internet.

Please help me to be patient with my computer... with the people I speak to at the help desks... those around me.

Help me to understand what I have to do.

Help me, Lord, right now and may the computer get sorted out soon, I pray!

131

Paperwork

Lord, why paperwork?

Proofreading, systems, meetings.

Did we ever live without these?

'I wonder if you could just...'

If someone else asks me this, I think I'll scream!

Lord, because you know everything, I thank you that you understand my frustration with paperwork; how it stops me doing what I see as my real job. Help!

Waiting

Lord, I seem to spend my whole life waiting...

Waiting for the bus or train

Waiting in the queue at the supermarket

Waiting for the traffic lights to change

Waiting for the exam results to come

Waiting for the computer to start

Waiting to see the children's teacher

Waiting to see the doctor

Waiting for the results of hospital tests.

Help me to use the time wisely, to pray for those around me – the supermarket staff, the other passengers on the bus or train, the local council who try to manage the traffic as best they can; for teachers, doctors, nurses, all hospital staff... and others in the community who keep things moving.

I want to wait *on* you, Lord, too, for direction. Guide my life – in its major direction as well as in the nitty-gritty details.

I put myself at your disposal again, Lord. I do want to serve you and others with my life, Lord, I pray. Amen.

Meal times

I thank you, heavenly Father, for the gift of this food before us. We thank you for those who have worked hard in preparing it.

We acknowledge you as the Giver of all things. May you bless this food to our bodies now so we may serve you even more fully.

May our conversation around the table be helpful and encouraging. In Christ's name we pray. Amen.

Marriage partner

Lord, I pray for my husband/wife. I thank you for them, for their love and care. As we look back, Lord, we thank you that you have been faithful to us; may we remain faithful to our marriage relationship.

May we grow in our love and respect for each other. May our trust deepen as the years go by, as we continue to share our lives with you and with each other. May we grow as a couple and also individually.

Give us good times together, Lord. Help us through the times that are more difficult, and the times when we take each other too much for granted.

Increase our tenderness, putting the other first. May we truly understand one another more, showing patience. Keep us really listening to each other. Help us deal with areas of conflict; may we continue to learn to express our love creatively.

May we cope with each other's weaknesses and insecurities, and encourage each other's strengths. Make us strong in you to face all our fears and hopes.

As we look to the future, Lord, may we place you at the centre of our marriage and may we serve you together. May our marriage become even stronger as we grow closer to you and each other. We pray in Jesus' name. Amen.

Being single

Lord, I thank you for the life you have given me. I thank you for the way you have created me, my individual character and personality.

Lord, I thank you for friends I am close to, those I can share my life with. I thank you for particular friends I can be especially close to, whom I can safely share my deepest thoughts with – everything about my life.

I thank you for times of fun and laughter, for times of deep thought and soul-searching, for parties and opportunities to express the kind of person you have made me to be.

Thank you for all the things I have been able to do and experience, places seen and explored, for adventures far and near, enjoying your great creation and different cultures and hospitality.

Lord, if you want me to meet a very special friend, one I am to spend the rest of my life with, I pray for that person right now, that we may find each other soon and may get to know each other well.

But until I find that special someone, Lord, may you use me and may I feel fulfilled in my daily life. I acknowledge you have an amazing plan for me whether I am single or married.

Please help me when I feel lonely, in the times when I do wonder about your plan for my life.

I pray in Christ's name. Amen.

Friends

Father, I thank you for friends: people I can be myself with, people who will stand by me through thick and thin.

I thank you for my friend's concern for me, asking, 'How are you *really* doing?' and being genuinely interested in my response.

I thank you that as friends we can grow together – sharing the same activities and experiences, the same outlook and understanding of life, similar memories, confidences, the same jokes.

May I be a true friend, too, listening, understanding, and responding to others with care and compassion.

But most of all I thank you for Christ, the friend who sticks closer than a brother who, even when I didn't want to know him or have anything to do with him, gave up his life for me. Lord, that is true sacrificial love. I thank you from the bottom of my heart for such an infinitely great commitment.

Thank you, Father, for friends. Amen.

Thanksgiving for past heroes of faith

Thank you, Lord, for spiritual giants: men and women who have gone before us, who have had hearts on fire for you, who have been bold in declaring Christ and living out his message.

May we imitate their stand for the truth, their passion for peace and justice, and their love for those who are forgotten and unlovely. May we imitate their faith, trusting you as they did.

We are thankful for those who helped us on our path of pilgrimage. May we lead lives of integrity and consistency, as they did.

In some ways our battles are the same as theirs, Lord – against sin, against the world, against Satan. Yet in other ways the battles are different, as sin and the devil express themselves differently. May we not be deceived but follow you constantly more and more closely.

May we be strong in you, wearing your full armour so that we can stand up to everything the devil throws at us.

May you continually be our vision, that we may trust in you fully to see us through, not depending on our own strength.

Lord, they are enjoying you fully now; may we have a foretaste of heaven, a passion to praise you and a deep desire to serve others where you have put us. In Jesus' name we pray. Amen.

Families

Lord, you understand all about families, the ups and downs of life, the hustle and bustle, the good times, the not-so-good times.

Father, I thank you for my family, for each member of it: my marriage partner and my children. Thank you for the variety you give us in our family – for our different characters, our individual strengths and weaknesses, for some who are quiet and some who are louder. May we all cope with one another and grow closer to one another and close to you.

Bless the times we are together as a family: may they be happy and secure times, times of fun, joy and laughter, times of loving – caring and sharing.

Be with us in the not-so-good times – times we find difficult, when we need to work harder at all living under the same roof. Give us all the strength and perseverance to pull together in the same direction.

May our life together as a family develop as we all get older; may our care and love for one another deepen and expand. May we continue to grow in the warmth and affection we have for one another. May all those who are members of my family come to know you personally and follow you.

May the bonds of trust and love go deep so that what we are as a family may be passed on to future generations. In Christ's name I pray. Amen.

Money

Lord, we have done the sums and we can't make sense of the figures. We've got more going out than coming in. Please help us to find a way through this. Help us to be realistic and work out a budget so that we can know how we can make ends meet and cope.

In Christ's name. Amen.

Leisure

Father, I thank you for the opportunity you give for rest. I remember, Lord God, that at the end of days of creation you rested. I remember, too, that the Lord Jesus went with his disciples to a quiet place to get some rest.

Lord, I pray that I may make wise of my use of free time. I recognize that it's not really 'free time', Lord; it's time you give me in which you want me to honour you, spending time with you by relaxing and being with friends, playing games and sports, pursuing hobbies and pastimes, enjoying being the individual you have made me to be. May I do things well, seeking to do what is good and commendable, not wasting the time you have given me.

Lord of all time, may I enjoy these hours and minutes you give, I pray in Jesus' name. Amen.

Sunday

Father, I thank you for this fantastic new day.

I thank you that I can come with your people to sing your praises and to declare your goodness.

Lord, the Bible says that if we come near to you, you will come near to us.

Help all of us who worship you today to know again the present reality of the living God. May we go deeper with you, each one of us, and together as a church.

Speak to us from your word, the Bible. Mould our thinking so that we will think your thoughts.

Give us *your light* for our journey, *your challenge* to our perceptions, and *your presence* to renew us.

Bring your fire to our hearts as we praise you; give your light to our minds as we hear your word.

Lord, make us sensitive to our voice; may we sense your presence with us; show us yourself afresh in Jesus Christ.

Inspire our prayers with your power as we receive again the emblems of your sacrifice, the bread and the wine, and may we be firmly reminded once more of the cost of our salvation.

Then, Lord, as we draw near to the end of our time together, may we put ourselves afresh at your disposal, making ourselves available to you again, so that you can use us just how, when and where you want to. When we have 'finished our service', as we put it, may our service really begin as we go back into your world equipped to show Christ to a needy world.

We ask all these prayers in Christ's name. Amen.

Communion

Lord, as we come to share in this simple meal, with you at the centre, as we take the bread and wine, may we recognize afresh your presence with us.

Heavenly Father, you are completely just and holy. You do not ignore our sins; in fact, you cannot, because your eyes are too pure to look at evil.

We are deeply aware that our sins have offended your righteousness and that we are no longer worthy to be called your children.

We can do nothing to blot out our sins. We can bring nothing to you; we can only cling to your cross.

We thank you that you have provided a way out. The penalty that we deserved to pay was paid by the Lord Jesus Christ himself on the cross. We thank you, Lord Jesus, that you gave up your life, you poured out your blood, to make us at one with yourself. Lord Jesus Christ, you took our place. You bore the punishment of the sins of the world in your own body... the punishment that was due to us. You laid down your life for us.

We trust in Christ's death for us right now, Father, and that you count us as righteous in your sight. We are forgiven, accepted in Christ. Thank you for the gift of faith you have given us. Thank you for Christ's death for us as the sign of your love for us. May we continue to lead a life of worship and service. We pray in Jesus' name. Amen.

Before a holiday

Lord, give us a good time on holiday.

Please give us safety as we travel, and a good relaxing time.

Lord, I pray that the time will be one of inner restoration. Renew us physically, emotionally and spiritually.

May we quickly unwind from all the strains, pressures, and tension – all the stress! – of our life and have an enjoyable time.

May we be refreshed as we enjoy new experiences, visit new places, make new friends, catch up with old friends.

May we have fun in the adventure before us – different activities or just chilling out – in all that we enjoy away from home and the ordinary routines of life.

If we worship you in unfamiliar surroundings, in a different style, may we able to express our adoration and praise and hear you speaking to us in a fresh way.

Thank you for this opportunity you have given, Lord, for us 'to get away from it all'.

May we return home refreshed – whole people again – to serve you and the community where you have put us.

May we not forget you as we go, but may we take you with us.

In Christ's name. Amen.

Flying

Lord, I don't like flying. I know it's the quickest way to get to my destination, but... the roar as the engines rev up to take off, the roller coaster as we rise into the sky, the unexpected turbulence that always seems to come just as I'm eating the snack or drinking coffee.

Help me, Lord, somehow to remain calm, I pray.

Help me to think of you, Lord Jesus, sitting next to me, and supporting the plane throughout its flight.

Please keep us safe, Lord! Amen.

149

At the end of a holiday

Lord, I'm not sure I really want to go back home.

We've had such a great time away that I don't think I want to face all the duties and responsibilities of going home and returning to work.

Thank you for the rest you have provided; I feel my batteries have been more or less fully recharged.

Thank you for fresh experiences, people I've met, new friends I've made, exciting places I've visited, different things I've become involved with.

May I not be overwhelmed by all that lies before me, but may I trust in you.

May I live in your power, in the power of your Spirit. May I know your help and presence now as I return home. I pray in Jesus' name. Amen.

7

Prayers Through the Year

New Year

Lord, I want to move on in my life in this coming year. At the moment, the new year is like a fresh notepad, empty and with nothing in it, no to-do lists, no scribble, nothing to mess it up.

May I not become preoccupied with the missed opportunities and wrongs of the past, but may I come to know Christ more deeply day by day.

But I also have to admit, Lord, that I am scared of what this new year might bring. I feel I don't have the resources within me for all that will come my way in the months ahead.

I thank you for the exciting things you have in store for me in the future. May I begin to dream your dreams for my life.

If this year brings its dark times, may I know your presence in those difficult days.

May I grow in my relationship with you this year. May I listen to you more closely and obey you more fully.

May I know your power within me each day to equip me to face the challenges that come.

Help me to trust in you, Lord, to keep focused on you, and to listen to your word. I give myself afresh to you now. Amen.

Lent

During these next weeks may I ponder my Lord Jesus even more closely.

Lord, I ask you to do a deeper work in me. Create in me a heart that is more sensitive to you.

Please conquer any remnants of a defiant, rebellious attitude in me. Refine me and make me more spiritually alert, more in tune with you.

But, Lord, I don't want to be preoccupied with my sin in these days of Lent. I want to be more taken up with Christ.

Give me a fresh vision of the Lord Jesus.

Enable me and equip me in these days to become more like Christ, I pray. Amen.

Mothering Sunday

On this Mother's Day, I thank you for my mother, her care, love and nurture over many years, in doing her best to bring me up. Thank you that she taught me what is important in life, for all her advice and warnings, and for the practical lessons I've learnt from her, for all the time spent on me and with me.

Thank you for her guidance, love and devotion, long before I was aware of it. Help me to be more grateful, I pray.

Mum, you gave me life; gave me directions; taught me right from wrong; advised me about friends.

Thank you, Lord, for my mother and her unconditional love. Amen.

Palm Sunday

On that first Palm Sunday, the children came celebrating your goodness, kindness and love, making way for you. They sang hosannas to you, Son of David, Son of God, Son of man.

You received the worship and praise of the crowds. As the King of glory passes our way, may we adore you with our hearts, speak about you with our lips, and serve you with our lives.

Lord, through this week, as the crowds turned against you, changing their 'Hosanna, hosanna' to 'Crucify, crucify' may I, with your help and in your power, stand up for you and remain faithful to you. Amen.

Good Friday

Lord, on this holy day we remember that you took all our sins away; you bore in your own body our sins upon the cross. You took the punishment, the guilt, the penalty that was due to us.

We do not know what pain you had to bear for us in those hours in which you were separated from your heavenly Father's love.

We are standing on holy ground as we ponder these truths.

We worship you that you did all this for your people, to be the Lamb of God who takes away the sin of the world, the spotless one who took on himself our guilt, our sin, our punishment.

Christ... the Son of God, who loved us and gave his life for us.

He has put us right with you, Father God. We have faith in you and that is credited to us as righteousness. Because of Christ's death on the cross, we are declared to be in a right relationship with you.

'Ransomed, healed, restored, forgiven' – what wonderful words, what amazing realities!

We worship you, heavenly Father, for the gift of your Son; that Christ loved us and gave himself up for us, to bring us back to God.

Thank you, heavenly Father, that today is not the end. Christ rose from the dead to prove that his sacrifice was accepted, to prove that he really is the Son of God.

He has redeemed us. We have been bought with a price. May we therefore live for you today, offering ourselves constantly to you, laying down our lives for others. We pray in the precious name of Christ. Amen.

Easter Day

'I know that my Redeemer lives.'

Wow!

I worship you, Lord Jesus Christ, for this amazing fact: that you came back to life and are alive right now.

That really is awesome!

158

Amidst all the questions I still have about life, one certainty rings out to every point in the universe: Christ is risen!

The immortal One has died for all sin and for all sinners in every time and in every place.

Christ has been brought back to life: surely this is the most thrilling victory of all time!

Lord Jesus Christ, you really are the Son of God.

I worship you in praise and adoration.

I give myself afresh to you right now on this day of all days.

Equip me with the power that raised Christ from the dead to serve you today and all the days ahead.

In Christ's name I pray. Amen.

Ascension Day

I thank you that you will come again to this earth, you will return in glory.

Lord Jesus Christ, I recall that on this day about 2,000 years ago, you returned to your heavenly Father.

Lord Jesus, receive honour, power and glory from me and all your people. All authority is now subject to you.

Thank you that you ascended to send your Holy Spirit and his gifts to us, and to prepare a place in heaven for us. You are now exalted in glory, praying for your people at the Father's side, ruling over all things.

May I know, even in my ordinary situation today, that I am (spiritually speaking) sitting with you in the heavenly realms.

Lift up my perspective on life to set my heart and mind firmly on the reality of heaven. May my mind be filled with thoughts of you and of the future when I really will be with you in glory. May I serve you more wholeheartedly, knowing your presence deep within me.

In Christ's name I pray.

Whitsun/Pentecost

Heavenly Father, we recall that on this day about 2,000 years ago, you poured out the gift of your Spirit on the disciples. We recall how that experience changed them completely, energizing them with your dynamic power so that they went out with the life-giving message of Christ.

We pray that today you would grip our lives afresh, bringing fire to our souls, giving us a new vision of Christ, of him dying for sinners and opening up the way to life. Exalt Christ as Lord and Saviour: his life, his death, his resurrection, his ascension.

Give us awe at your presence. Deepen our appreciation of the love of God. Come in your power, Spirit of God, and change the hearts and lives of many, even this day. May we not put the brakes on the move of your Spirit. May we know showers of blessings upon us as we come together in the powerful name of Jesus Christ.

Refresh us with the sweet dew of your presence, so we bear lasting fruit, not simply producing early blossom. Restore us, renew us inwardly. May we be open to a fresh movement of your Spirit. May we catch the fire again!

Release in us that joy and freedom that come directly from your Spirit.

Come with your healing touch. Give us that Pentecostal power of Christ to turn the world upside down, back to right way up.

Tear down every obstacle and barrier to the fire of your Spirit. Move us on with you – do whatever it takes to move us on with you. May we really meet with the living God.

If necessary, Lord, put a 'spiritual bomb' under us, to get us going for you, to wake us up to the realities of life and death, of heaven and hell.

Lord, we want everyone in our generation to hear about Christ, to meet with him for themselves. Equip us to be vibrant people who display the reality of Jesus Christ in our lives; we pray in his name. Amen.

Father's Day

Thank you, Lord God, for my father. Thank you for his care, guidance and support.

Thank you that he did what he thought best in bringing me up, that he showed me what he thought was right and important in life, and trained me to do it.

Thank you for the freedom I was given, all his words of advice and warning, for the practical lessons I've learnt from him.

Thank you for fun times with him.

Thank you, Lord, for my father. Amen.

Harvest thanksgiving

On this special day, heavenly Father, we remember that you are the Giver of all things. We may plough the fields and scatter the seed, but we acknowledge you are the One who gives growth.

We give thanks to you, for you have been good to us. You have provided us with plenty. We have tasted your goodness and sing for joy at the works of your hands.

We are sorry that we take your work of caring for this world too much for granted. We go to the superstores, expecting to find all kinds of fruits and vegetables the whole year round. We forget the work of farmers who have patiently sown the seed and nurtured the growing plants in all weathers throughout the year.

We acknowledge again, heavenly Father, our dependence on others in our community and, above all, on you, the One who gives life to, and sustains, all things.

You have blessed this world with crops. In your goodness, you have provided us with plenty. But we also remember the many parts of the world that do not know your abundance – areas of drought and famine, of conflict, of floods, of deep need. We pray for our friends who are seeking to bring justice, fair trade and a balance to the lives of people in the rich and poor nations of this world, that you will help them, so that we will live as one vibrant community in this, your world.

Amen.

Remembrance Day

Dear Lord and Father of all, we come to you on this solemn day of remembrance.

We recall the lives of those who made the ultimate sacrifice for their country, so that we would know freedom from injustice, tyranny and oppression. We will not forget them.

We thank you for the determination and the courage of those who laid down their lives that others might live. We will not forget them.

We pray your comfort for those families and friends who lost dear ones in battles, conflicts and war. Be with them in their pain and grief. May the thought that they did not die in vain bring strength and encouragement in their sorrow. We pray in the name of our risen Lord, Jesus Christ. Amen.

Thanksgiving

Father in heaven, we come at this time to thank you for your goodness toward us as a family. We recognize your mercy, grace and favour to us.

We come with thankfulness in our hearts to worship you. We thank you for blessing us as a family. We acknowledge you as the One who has given us so many good things. We want to share with others in need, too, Lord.

We pray your peace and wholeness for us and all families on this, your earth. We celebrate the diversity of people that you have made, and we gladly acknowledge our Saviour and Lord of all, the Lord Jesus Christ, in whose name we pray. Amen.

165

Bible Sunday

Heavenly Father, we thank you from the depths of our beings for your written word, the Bible.

We thank you that it points so clearly to the living Word himself, our Lord Jesus Christ.

We thank you that you inspired the writers of your word. We thank you for your word's authority. We declare again that we want to submit our lives to its commands.

We thank you for those who sacrificed their lives so that we might have your word in our own language.

We pray for those engaged in the task of translating your word into all the languages of this, your world. Give them strength in this task. Renew their vision, that one day people from every ethnic group will stand before the throne in the presence of the Lamb.

We pray for all those who seek to explain, teach and preach your word, that you will give light to their minds and make their hearts sensitive and responsive to you. May they not silence or quieten the word of God, but may they unleash its power.

We pray that we will all continue to delight in your word and, as we respond in obedience, may you make us wise, so that we come to know salvation through Jesus Christ, and become mature, fully equipped to be fruitful in your service. Amen.

Advent

At this time of year, I thank you that Christmas is drawing near – the time when we celebrate the coming of God into the world in human form... born as a baby in a dirty, smelly shed, ignored and despised by most, and welcomed and worshipped by a few.

Lord, may I take time to prepare myself for your coming. Take away everything that gets in the way of a simple life that is clearly focused on you. Have your way in me. May you have smooth access to the depths of my being.

So, Lord, even amidst all the shopping, the countdown to the 'last shopping days before Christmas' may I not forget the fact that it really is all about you. I pray in Jesus' name. Amen.

Christmas Day

So the big day has finally come – all the excitement, all the preparation, all the presents (no shopping days left before Christmas!), all the cards... all the lists, all the little piles of presents and cards for nephews and nieces, aunts and uncles, and then, I almost forgot...

Hey, hang on a moment, aren't I forgetting what Christmas is really all about?

Lord, today is such a celebration of the greatest fact of all, that God broke into human history – the human story – in the person of Christ.

You loved the world so much that you left the glory of heaven to come to this corrupt and dusty earth to be born as a baby, to grow up as a boy, to become an adolescent and then a man... all for us, for *me*, to show us the Father, to bring us back to God.

May I also reflect your spirit and attitude this day and through the year, being humble, not insisting on my rights, but serving others.

Yes, Lord, I greet you, 'born this happy morning'. I give you glory. Come to my heart afresh even this today: may I not just squeeze you in among everything else today, but may you be the centre of everything. Amen.

End of the year

Father, as this year draws to a close, I want to look back over it with you – its twists and turns, its high points and low points.

I thank you for how you have looked after me this year, your goodness and strength and all that you have helped me achieve. I am also saddened that I have neglected opportunities that you have given me. I am sorry for those occasions when I have wasted time. Forgive me for those times, Lord, when I have not loved you as I should have. Cleanse me once again from my sin.

169

As the new year dawns, may I respond ever more deeply to your love. Give me a fresh vision of Christ. May my worship be deeper. May your word be even more important to me. May I set my heart even more firmly on pilgrimage. I pray in Christ's name. Amen.

8

Prayers on Special Occasions

Wedding *(see chapter 2, page 43)*

A new home *(see chapter 2, page 45)*

Birth *(see chapter 2, page 46)*

Wedding anniversary

Heavenly Father, on this anniversary of the day when we first promised ourselves to each other, we thank you for your faithfulness that has enabled us to be faithful to each other.

We thank you that you have provided for us along every step of our journey, that you have been with us in the sad times and joyful occasions, in our dreams, our hopes and our fears.

As we look back over the years we see how our love for each other has blossomed, our friendship for each other has deepened and our trust in each other has become stronger. We thank you that with your help we belong to each other even more firmly than we did when we first got married.

We pray, Lord, that in the years to come we will grow even closer to each other and to you, Lord, that we might serve you together in happiness all the days of our life.

In Jesus' name we pray. Amen.

Dedication of children

Lord Jesus, we remember how you welcomed children into your presence.

Lord, today we thank you for [child's name], we thank you for the gift of life. We thank you for the safe birth and good health of this child. We thank you for all the potential within this young life.

We thank you for the precious gift of this child. We pray for their parents, that you will give them love, patience and wisdom as they give themselves to you in bringing up this little one; give them good health, many years of fun and laughter as a family.

We pray for this child's safety, Lord, in this world. Please keep them secure in the love of family, friends, church and the wider community.

We pray that in due course, Lord, this little one will come to know Christ as their own personal Lord and Saviour. We pray in Christ's name. Amen.

Christening (infant baptism)

Lord Jesus Christ, as we bring this child to you now, we recall how you took children into your arms to bless them.

We thank you for the great gifts of life and health that we acknowledge come from you. We welcome this little one into the family of your church. As we as parents and godparents make promises on behalf of this child, we pray you will keep them secure in your love and that in due course this young one will know the truth of these promises. As we commit ourselves to bring up this child to follow you, we pray that they will personally come to know all the promises of Christ in their own lives. In the name of Jesus Christ we pray. Amen.

First communion (child)

I thank you for today, Lord Jesus.

Lord Jesus, I come to you this day to thank you that you died for me.

As I take the bread and the wine, I want to thank you, Jesus, that you loved me so much you died on the cross for me.

I pray that today will be the first step of the adventure of knowing and trusting you more and more day by day. Amen.

First communion (parent)

Heavenly Father, as our child takes communion for the first time today, we thank you that you have brought us all to this day.

We pray that as they receive the bread and the wine, they may touch and taste the reality of Christ himself. May they know in their hearts that Christ died for them. May they have great joy as they begin their adventure of life with you. We pray this in Christ's name. Amen.

Starting school

(see chapter 2, page 48)

Starting at a new school

(see chapter 2, page 49)

Baptism (believers')

Lord, as I am baptized today, I thank you for the adventure of new life that I have begun.

I thank you that I know that Christ died for my sins, that I share with him in his death and resurrection.

I thank you for the pictures of baptism, that as I am under the water my old life is finished with; that as I come up again, I rise to new life in Christ.

May I always remember I am a new person in Christ, that the controlling power of sin in my life has been broken, that I am one of your children and that you are my heavenly Father. May I know the full power and presence of the Holy Spirit, filling and guiding me every day.

I pray for my friends and family who watch me being baptized, that they will not only be happy for me but will also want to follow Christ for themselves.

Lord, be honoured today as I follow you in obedience. May this step be the first of many steps that lead to growth and maturity in Christ.

Amen.

Confirmation

Heavenly Father, I thank you that you have led me to this day in my life. Confirm in me the promises made on my behalf at my christening,

I thank you that you give me joy, that you have kept me safe and you have provided for me.

I acknowledge that I am a sinner, but I thank you that I can equally confess Jesus Christ as my own Saviour.

I now trust in Christ's death to save me, and in his risen power to uphold me.

Strengthen me with your Spirit; sustain me when I am tempted to doubt or to go astray. May you constantly remind me that I am one of your children. I pray that I will come to know Christ more and more every day of my life, for I pray this in his name. Amen.

Birthday (1)

Lord Jesus, I thank you for the sheer privilege of knowing you. I thank you that you bring me into the Father's presence.

I thank you that you have given me life, breath and everything this last year – that you have provided for all my needs. I freely admit that I have not loved you as I should have; I have not followed you as closely as I should have. Please forgive me and cleanse me again, I pray.

I pray for new challenges this year, that I may live to bring you praise, that I may realize afresh that I live to worship and adore you.

I pray, too, that as I bask in the sunshine of your love, I may delight even more to do your will, to grow in you to depths I cannot even imagine.

I pray very much too, that my love for others will become wider and more generous. May I become more like Christ in the days ahead. May I learn to accept whatever you bring my way this year. May I seek to bring Christ and his kingdom of peace, justice and righteousness to your world.

Lord, may I recapture a sense of the wonder and adventure of life. It seems I have only just begun to experience the fullness of your creation, the whole rainbow that makes up what it means to be human. May I explore with you and with others what it means to celebrate the joys of being one of your children. In Jesus' name. Amen.

Birthday (2)

Almighty God and heavenly Father, as I look back over another year that you have kept me by your grace, I thank you that you have provided for me and have sustained me.

I thank you for your mercy and grace toward me. I am amazed that you still concern yourself with me.

I thank you for the cross of Christ, for the constant power of the blood of Christ, bringing forgiveness for my sins that I confess to you.

I thank you, too, for all that I have learnt – about you, your word, your world and myself.

I thank you for family and friends – for getting to know long-standing friends more, and coming to know new friends.

Lord, as I look ahead to this new year with you, I pray that I would grow more like Jesus Christ in his compassion, holiness and justice. Challenge me, I pray, this year to go on even more deeply with you, to follow you more closely, to love you more fully... and may I learn to trust you even more. Release your power through me, and may I learn to lead a life that is more fully human.

May your word become increasingly important to me. May I set my heart even more firmly on pilgrimage.

I pray in Jesus' name. Amen.

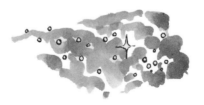

Starting university

(see chapter 2, page 50)

Graduation

(see chapter 2, page 51)

New job

(see chapter 2, page 52)

On your second marriage

Heavenly Father, we thank you for this day. You know we have been looking forward to today.

Thank you for your presence here in our joy and celebration.

Thank you that we know that you are Lord of all life. Thank you for new beginnings... a fresh start and renewed opportunities to serve you in life. Thank you that you use our past experiences to mould us to be stronger people to serve you more fully in this world.

We thank you for each other, for bringing us together. Be with us today in the promises we make. May we know you are with us as we speak out our love, respect and commitments to each other. Watch over us and protect us as we seek to fulfil them day by day.

May we remember this day as special for the rest of our lives.

In all our excitement about our love, may we not forget you, heavenly Father, the Giver of life and love, but help us to draw closer to you, too.

May today be so important and the beginning of the fulfilment of our hopes and dreams. In Jesus' name and for his sake, we pray. Amen.

Retreat

As we go on retreat, Lord, we pray that we may sense your presence. May we realize again your awesome presence, your majesty, your holiness, your mercy and your grace. As we leave behind the hustle and bustle of our ordinary lives, may we become still enough to sense the ripples of your Spirit touching the inner recesses of our lives.

Lord, in our time away we want to set our hearts on pilgrimage. Strengthen us as we wait on you.

Spirit of the living God, show us Christ anew. Put the searchlight on our lives, Lord; humble us so that we see Christ afresh. May we realize again that we are nothing, but Christ is all. Bring us to a deeper repentance, a fresh love for Christ, and a more emphatic resolve to serve you in your power.

May we know more of your grace flowing into our lives. Pour out your love even more deeply into our hearts.

May we return not only refreshed, but also with a clearer vision of your plans for our lives. As we come away from our retreat, may the love you have put in our hearts spill out into the dry and needy community where we live and work. May we declare by our words and our actions the power of Christ's risen life.

In Christ's name we pray. Amen.

9

Prayer as a Relationship
with God

Coming near to God

O God, you who are without beginning or end, you who are everywhere and in everything, I come to you, even though I am not always sure of your reality.

I am amazed that you should bother with human beings who are often so unconcerned about the great issues of life and eternity. We get so caught up in the mundane things of life, such as watching television and what food to cook tonight.

Yet you are almighty God; you are the mystery beyond all mysteries; no one can compare with you. You are above all things. You created all things. You do not fade at all but always remain strong.

Help me to know you more deeply, trust you more fully, and follow you more closely, I pray. Amen.

Coming to know Jesus Christ

Lord God, I come into your presence. I admit I have broken your law, that there is a deep selfishness within me, that by myself I cannot love you as I should. I realize my personal need of Jesus Christ.

I turn away from everything that is wrong in my life. I am truly sorry that I have not lived life your way but mine.

I thank you, Lord, that in your great love you have made the way open for me to come back to you. I realize that it is only the cross of Christ that can bring me back to you. I want to respond to your goodness.

I thank you that Jesus Christ died on the cross for me. Give me faith to believe that Christ died on the cross to forgive *my* sin, to take on himself the punishment due to me, and to make me clean from all the guilt of my sin.

I trust my whole life to you. I humbly yet confidently look to Christ right now. Come to me as my Saviour to rescue me from death and hell. Come to me as my Lord to direct my life toward God and heaven.

I want to give my whole being – my heart, mind and will – to you, Lord Jesus, right now. Jesus Christ, I take you to be my God. I want to follow you for the rest of my life. Amen.

Following Jesus Christ

Lord Jesus Christ, I thank you for the invitation you give to all to follow you. Lord, I hear your voice, *but...*

Lord, I want to be honest with you: I'm finding it difficult to submit to you right now. I sense you clearly putting your finger on areas of my life that I'm hanging onto.

I'm afraid you'll ask me to do things I don't want to, give up things I'm holding onto, and ask me to go to places I don't want to go to.

Lord, break down my resistance, my opposition, the obstacles I'm putting between you and me.

But actually, Lord, all these reasons and excuses are petty and trivial – they pale into insignificance compared with the all-surpassing worth of knowing you.

Lord, I realize there is a cost in following you. Please give me strength, help and courage so that I may rise to the challenge of becoming a true disciple. I pray in your precious name. Amen.

Knowing God

Father, I thank you for the sheer privilege of knowing you. I worship and adore you that you have revealed yourself to me, given me the gift of faith, caught me up into your purposes... that I can listen to you day by day and seek to live out your purposes as I follow you in this world.

Lord Jesus Christ, I praise you that you are my Saviour and Lord, my Master, the One who gives my life purpose and meaning. Thank you that you died on the cross for me, that you took all my sins upon yourself. Thank you for your glorious resurrection that declared you to be truly the Son of God. Thank you that you are seated at the Father's side, praying for me right now. You are the centre of my life, my compass, the One who gives my whole being direction.

Lord Jesus Christ, I want to know you, to love you and to enjoy you.

May I know in my experience what is true in theory, that I am united with Christ. When he died, I died; when he was raised from the dead, so was I.

May I truly know within me the power of the risen, living Christ. May I know in my life that the controlling power of sin has come to an end, has been broken, because of Christ's death.

Precious Holy Spirit, I thank you for your role in constantly pointing me to Christ. Thank you for revealing the wrong within my heart and life, my need of a Saviour. I am so grateful for the deep sense of assurance you give me. You have given me faith; you have subdued my defiant and corrupt heart and have brought me back to Christ. Fill me afresh with yourself, Holy Spirit.

Father, Son, Spirit, may I show what you are truly like by serving others in this, your world. May I continue to know you more, worshipping you, receiving your touch to answer my needs, helping me in my weaknesses. May I submit to you and obey you even more deeply, to become more like you. May I show what you are truly like by serving others in this, your world, affirming individuals as made in your image, and showing them your goodness by how I lead my life. In Christ's name I pray. Amen.

Listening to God

Lord, how can I discern your voice?

Everyone tells me I will hear you speaking, but I don't seem to very often.

As I read your word, I pray with all my heart that I will truly listen to what your Spirit is saying.

Lord, underline, highlight, emphasize the parts you particularly want me to take to heart.

In the quiet, may I hear your voice of stillness, reassurance, but also, Lord, I pray, of challenge.

May I not miss the clear and direct challenges of your word. Help me to submit to them and obey them, whether I feel like doing so or not.

Lord, quieten my inner being to be still enough to respond to you. May I listen with a sensitive heart that is quick to trust you in obedience. In Jesus' name I pray. Amen.

191

Knowing the power of the cross

Heavenly Father, I thank you for the cross of Christ. I cannot possibly fully understand the full meaning of the death of Christ for the sins of the world, but I know…

… that all my sin was laid on him

… that the punishment for my sin was taken by him

… that the guilt of my sin was put on him

… that I have been redeemed, pardoned, acquitted, forgiven

… that I, who once was your enemy, have been brought near, have been brought home, to God, to be your child and your friend

… that Satan was defeated on the cross, that he was robbed of his power

… that sin no longer controls me, because I am now ruled by the Lord Jesus Christ himself.

I confess again my sins, and turn away from them, believing that Christ died for me. Make and keep me pure within.

As I ponder the power of the cross again, may I be lost afresh in wonder, love and praise. May I know again that I have been crucified with Christ, that the life I now lead is the outflow of his life in and through me to this your needy world.

May I follow your example and deny myself, taking up your cross daily as I follow you. May I show that I know something of the power of the cross in how I live for you, boldly and passionately bringing the message of the cross to others.

May I live even today in absolute certainty that I am your child.

May I continue to learn to follow Christ today, remembering that his death and glorious resurrection is the doorway to new life, opening up the way to move beyond the ordinary, to live a new life for you today, for you and your glory.

In Jesus' name I pray. Amen.

Depending on the Holy Spirit

Lord, we cry out for more of your Spirit, the Spirit of God, the Spirit of Christ himself. Spirit of God, we come to you now.

Focus our lives again on your glory and power, all that you are. Bring us back completely to Christ and the good news. Lift us up from the mere ordinary routines of simply existing... even for you. Inspire us once more with yourself.

Reawaken in us a sense of God and his holiness; deepen the sense of your presence. Make us more responsive to your Spirit-inspired word. Make us more sensitive toward the corruption in our own hearts.

Re-energize our souls with your sense of the beauty of Christ himself.

May we come to know Jesus Christ more, appreciate his life and ministry afresh, look again at his teachings, his touch, his healings, his miracles. Scatter the mist, take the veil from our faces to see him more clearly. As we consider him, may we sense a great glory that will lead us to fall down on our knees in wonder, love and praise.

Fill us – me – each one of us with an overflow of your precious Holy Spirit. May he lead us to know Christ more in our hearts. Then, Lord, may we not only bask in the glorious sunshine of your love, but also follow you more closely, and take you to the needy world around us.

May the flow of the Spirit within us be released beyond the limits we place on you so that we are more fully equipped to serve you in our communities.

In Jesus' name we pray. Amen.

Growing in Christian character

Lord, I want to know Jesus more. I know him just a little; I want to grow in my knowledge of him. But I don't just want to know *about* him, I want to come closer to him, to think his thoughts, to see people and situations through his eyes, to have his love and compassion.

May I become more like Jesus Christ. May my walk with him be more consistent. May my life show wholeness and integrity.

Lord, may I know the help of your Spirit to make me more like Jesus Christ. May I cultivate the fruit of your Spirit:

love, joy, peace

patience, kindness, goodness

faithfulness, gentleness and self-control.

Lord, where I am stubborn and resist you and your purposes for my life, knock the sharp edges off my life. Mould me to become your true child, while I am still in your presence. Shape me, so that I am sensitive and responsive to you. May Christ be formed within me.

Help me to discern your way, Lord Jesus, I pray, and give me the courage to follow it. In his name I pray. Amen.

Longing for God

Lord, you are all we want. We long for you with our whole beings.

Lord God, we want to enjoy you, to experience again your fullness, to bathe in the ocean of your love.

We long to see Jesus, to gaze on the beauty of the Lord, to contemplate his glory. Melt our hearts again to be saturated afresh with an even deeper, fuller, more joyful sense of your presence.

As we realize how securely Christ holds our lives, may we lay hold of him by faith even more firmly.

Give us hearts that have undivided loyalty, hearts that are wholly set on you.

We pray that we will come to know Jesus Christ even more deeply, that our hearts will delight more fully to act on your commands, putting them into practice to bring Christ to this world.

May our passion for you become even stronger, even deeper and even more focused.

May we cultivate the fruit of your Spirit, growing in love, joy, peace, patience, kindness, goodness, faithfulness, gentleness and self-control.

Lord, all these are big requests, but we thank you that you are a big God, that nothing is impossible with you.

We need all the powerful resources of your Spirit for all that you are leading us into.

Lord, we long for you so that we will give glory, honour and praise. We long for you so that we will become the people you want us to be in Christ, to realize our full potential in him. Lord, we pray for your kingdom to come. We long for you so that we may effectively take the good news of Jesus Christ to every part of your world. Amen.

Looking forward to Christ's second coming

Lord Jesus, I thank you for the certain promise that Christ will come again, that one day you will return to earth.

One day, the story of this world will come to an end. One day, there will be no more tears, no injustice, no more death, no more suffering. One day, we will know you fully. One day, your people will be completely free from sin.

Lord, until that day comes, may I stay alert. May I expect the unexpected, leading a life of integrity as I wait for that day.

Lord, I thank you for the patience you show the world, that you are not willing that anyone should die not knowing you. You want everyone to turn back to you and come to know you. May I therefore be bold in living for you and making known the good news of Jesus Christ to those around me.

One day you are coming, Lord Jesus,

O glorious day!

Come quickly, Lord Jesus. Amen.

Index